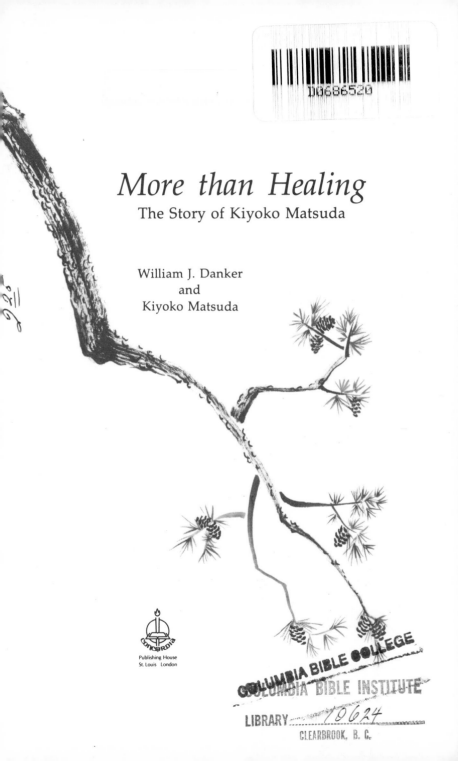

More than Healing
The Story of Kiyoko Matsuda

William J. Danker
and
Kiyoko Matsuda

Concordia
Publishing House
St. Louis London

Concordia Publishing House, St. Louis, Missouri
Concordia Publishing House Ltd., London E. C. 1
Copyright © 1973 Concordia Publishing House
Library of Congress Catalog Card No. 73-78105
ISBN 0-570-03161-3

MANUFACTURED IN THE UNITED STATES OF AMERICA

*To all who suffer
and to those who love them*

Acknowledgments

Japanese award a very low esteem to an *on o shiranai kata*, a person who fails to recognize obligation.

We should be such an *on o shiranai kata*, if we failed to acknowledge the help we have received from many quarters in telling the story of Kiyoko Matsuda's heroic faith and witness.

There was first her own magnificent achievement in writing down her story in the last year of her life, in spite of pain, weakness, and advanced age.

We thank Jaroslav Vajda of Concordia Publishing House for encouragement and guidance. Luther D. Kistler, as well as Carol and Paul Kreyling, three who knew Kiyoko Matsuda well, provided much assistance. Among those who read the manuscript and counselled us were Pierce and Wilma Beaver, Florence Montz, president of the Lutheran Women's Missionary League, Janie McCutchen, acting executive secretary of the Board for Women's Work in the Presbyterian Church, U. S., Neva Merzlok, Margaret Dannevik, Lois Dankenbring, and Delmar Glock.

The Missionary Research Library of New York, Concordia Seminary Library of St. Louis, Katherine Hockin and Gwen R. P. Norman of Toronto were friends in need. Ken Gerike tracked down necessary references. Takeshi Miyamoto of Matsue, and Masao Shimodate of Omiya, Japan, graduate students at Concordia Seminary, St. Louis, were valued consultants on things Japanese. Our daughter,

Elizabeth Mann, M. D., advised us on Chapter X. The special efforts of Concordia's secretarial staff enabled Mrs. Matsuda to read her life story on the very eve of her passing.

We are indebted to Harold G. Henderson's excellent *Introduction to Haiku* (Garden City, N.Y.: Doubleday, 1958) for some of the translations of Japanese verse. Others were the joint work of the authors.

William J. Danker

Contents

Aki fukaki tonari wa

nani wo suru hito zo?

Nearing autumn's close,

my neighbor, now—what is it

that she does?

—Matsuo Basho (1644—1694)

CHAPTER ONE

Reunion in Tokyo

There was something familiar about the eyes, though they had clearly known suffering since we had parted fourteen years earlier. Through the windows one could see that our old friend still lived there and that her love for us was unchanged. But otherwise the earthly house in which she lived was terribly altered. Her once black hair was white as the wings of a crane. Unusually tall and large for a Japanese woman, she seemed taller than ever in spite of shoulders that were bowed. For she had lost a great deal of weight and was poignantly slender.

But what shocked not only me but also my wife and daughter, who had joined me in Tokyo, was her face. It was so changed and disfigured that we could barely recognize her. Her appearance had been altered, but not the way the face of a city changes gradually in times of peace. No, it was like the change that had come to the face of Tokyo when it was bombed in World War II. I had seen that devastated face of the bombed and burned-out capital as my C-54 plane circled to land at Haneda airport in 1948, when I arrived as a missionary. The countenance of this woman before us looked like that.

Dear God, her entire lower jawbone was missing!

Gone the once strong jaw! Gone the firm good looks! Now she looked for all the world like that comic strip figure of another generation—Andy Gump. But there was nothing comical about this apparition. We could see only tragedy.

This was Kiyoko Matsuda. In the early years of launching a brand-new mission enterprise in postwar Japan, she had been first my personal secretary and then a staff member of our Japan Lutheran Hour, which grew to be the largest radio Gospel ministry in Japan, with 117 stations. Outstanding in her ability to understand, read, speak, and write English, Matsuda-san had been a valuable co-worker and friend. I recalled how she had interpreted for me on one occasion when I had addressed 400 women in a provincial town as they knelt ladylike on a hard wooden floor. She had also interpreted some of my regular monthly addresses to the 200 officers of what *Reader's Digest* termed "the largest woman's club in the world" at Yokosuka, Japan.

With sure feminine instinct, Matsuda-san was making the most of a Japanese custom that enabled her to hide the worst of her disfigurement. Over her mouth she wore the gauze mask that has been in vogue in crowded Japan ever since the deadly worldwide influenza epidemic in 1919. Visitors to Japan are quick to notice these surgical masks looped over the ears and chins of many Japanese people today, especially in winter. The basic theory is that they are to inhibit the catching or the giving of colds and respiratory diseases. After the first thirty minutes' use their efficiency is said to be dubious.

Kiyoshi Hasegawa, now professor of English at Ochanomizu National Women's University in Tokyo, was my houseboy when I first arrived in Tokyo. Then a student at Rikkyo University, he had lost one eye in wartime bombing. But his vision in the other could be acute.

With a smile, he explained: "You see, if a girl doesn't

11

have pretty teeth, then she may wear the gauze mask more often."

But with Matsuda-san's entire lower jawbone missing, the effort to cover the destruction of her face was more pathetic than successful. And when she loosened the loop over one ear to try to converse with us, we glimpsed the lower lip shrunken to the shape of a bird's beak. Matter-of-factly she informed us that she existed entirely on a liquid diet. She was not able to swallow so much as an aspirin. The functioning of the throat had been much impaired.

Matsuda-san was a challenge to my personal faith. She was causing me to think deeply.

I had just returned from a journey of many weeks visiting the headquarters of many of the so-called new religions in Japan. These have mushroomed since the war. The old Shinto gods had been exploited by the militarists in a fanatic do-or-die struggle that had convulsed China. Japan's armed forces had invaded Southeast Asia and the islands of the South Sea to the doorstep of Australia. This paroxysm had cost millions of lives and one quarter of the total national treasure of Japan.

After the surrender in 1945 Japan lay prostrate in total defeat. People were questioning themselves, their most cherished cultural values, and their inherited religious faith. With their cities and houses destroyed, widespread joblessness, poverty, and hunger, the people were seeking immediate help to get through the pressing problems that each day brought.

Many missionaries and their supporters had expected Christianity to fill the much-discussed "religious vacuum" in postwar Japan.

But to the surprise and consternation of many, it was the "new religions" that filled the gap. They offered people salvation for their troubles in the here and now: success instead of failure, healing in place of disease. Instead of pie in the sky, they promised benefits on earth. All things were possible, if only one had faith. If one failed to overcome failure and disease, this simply proved that one lacked sufficient faith. Such people found themselves twofold failures and doubly depressed.

Yet multitudes were seeking salvation by the power of positive thinking as espoused by the new religions. Best known outside Japan is perhaps the Soka Gakkai, the "Value-Creating Society," ebullient lay movement among Nichiren Buddhists. At Taisekiji, their "Great Stone Temple" at the base of Mount Fuji, I had seen 15,000 pilgrims per day streaming through this great temple complex seeking answers to their prayers: perhaps success in love or business or, possibly, healing from disease. From a membership of 1,500 in 1945 Soka Gakkai has exploded to a present level of more than 5 million, according to the most conservative estimates. Their own public relations department claims 15 million.

From such triumphal, success-oriented, this-worldly religion I had come back to a small part of the Christian church in Japan. More than four centuries after Francis Xavier, the first Christian missionary, arrived in 1549, it still numbers only about one million baptized members.

From the many who claimed miracles of healing through the endless repetition of *Myoho Rengekyo* — "Hail to the *Lotus sutra!*" — I returned to a woman who had prayed to Jesus Christ for many years through ten surgical operations and had not been healed. Instead, she had lost her entire lower jawbone. Was the *Lotus sutra* more powerful than the Christian Bible? Did the Soka Gakkai have a right to succeed in its vaunted boast to win first one third of Japan and then millions of people throughout the world to the Buddhist doctrines of Nichiren, nationalistic reformer of 700 years ago? Was God punishing her for some unconfessed sins?

But in that unforgettable reunion with Matsuda-san in the very building where once we had worked together, I discovered that Jesus Christ had endowed her with more than physical healing. And that makes her story worth telling.

Furusato ya yoru mo

sawaru mo

bara no hana.

The place where I was born:

all I come to—all I touch—

blossoms of the thorn.

—Issa (1762–1826)

CHAPTER TWO

An Old-Fashioned Grandmother

It was a humid August night in the quiet country town of Ota about fifty miles north of Tokyo in Ibaraki Prefecture. The heat of the eighth month was so oppressive that the people found themselves longing for the typhoon season in spite of its dangers, because it would bring cooler weather and the famed *Nihonbare*, the clear blue autumn skies of Japan.

In an old substantial thatched house a young wife lay in hard labor with her first child. The beads of sweat stood out on her brow under the soft glow of the *chochin*, the Japanese lantern. But even when the waves of pain reached their highest crest, the young mother made no sound. Outside, a cicada shrilled away its short life. Like the long line of women stretching back before her into the shadows of the centuries, the youthful mother was a true daughter of the samurai. From one of her warrior lineage, the grandmother and the midwife had expected no other behavior.

The first cry the servants heard beyond the paper sliding doors was the thin, treble wail of a little black-haired baby girl. Her parents named her Kiyoko. From her earliest shaping the Creator was equipping her for the stern tests of the future.

It was 1891, the 24th year of the Meiji era. Less than a quarter century earlier, a 15-year-old boy had ascended the throne. With his reign the policy of Japan's 250-year-old isolation from the rest of the world had ended. Modernization, catching up under forced draught with the rest of the world, became the order of the day. Such acceleration of change as even Europe and America have never known struck Japan with the violence of a typhoon as Japan raced to make up 250 lost years. The lives of little Kiyoko and her entire family were tossed about like cockleshells on the turbulent currents of the new times.

The Western child is One in a family. The Oriental child is one in a Family. To understand Matsuda-san it is essential to know something of her ancestry.

"My mother was born of a medical family," Matsuda-san recalls. "Both her father and her grandfather were physicians, though very different in type. Her grandfather belonged to the old school of Chinese medicine, while her father was one of the very few doctors trained in Western medicine in those secluded days before the Meiji era."

One may wonder how he could possibly study Western medicine in a time when Japanese people were forbidden under pain of death to travel abroad.

The only contact with foreigners permitted by the Tokugawa family during the long years when they controlled all Japan, including the emperor, was at Nagasaki on Kyushyu, southernmost of Japan's four main islands. The Dutch were the only nation permitted to trade with Japan for more than two centuries. But even this contact was carefully regulated. Only one ship a year was allowed to call. The Dutch were permitted to maintain a trading station with a permanent settlement on the manmade island of Dejima connected with Nagasaki by a causeway. But they had to remain on this tiny island and could not so much as set foot on the soil of Japan proper.

"My mother's father was sent to Nagasaki," Kiyoko-san relates, "to study medicine under the guidance of Dutch professors. That was a magnificent opportunity in those days before the Meiji Restoration of 1868. Perhaps a little like being chosen as an astronaut to the moon today. Certainly it was much rarer than the chance to study abroad nowadays. You can understand therefore what an exceptional and promising young doctor my grandfather was in his day."

Matsuda-san's grandfather was born of a long line of doctors who served the *daimyo*, the feudal lord of Nihonmatsu in Fukushima Prefecture in the northern part of Honshu, Japan's main island. He was later adopted by his uncle, Rekisenin Oka, a court physician of the *daimyo* Rekko, feudal lord of Mito, in Ibaraki Prefecture. Rekko was a very powerful noble because of his family connections with one of the three branches of the Tokugawa family.

"My grandmother often told us," Matsuda-san remembers, "that Rekisenin Oka, who had adopted her husband, was a favorite court physician of Rekko, the *daimyo* of Mito. But unfortunately he became involved in the wholesale roundup of the Ansei Era (1854 — 1860)."

For more than two centuries the Tokugawa *shoguns*, who ruled Japan in place of the emperor, had excluded all foreigners. That policy, known as *sakoku* and formally decreed in 1639, had isolated Japan from intercourse with the family of nations. It had also preserved the supremacy of the Tokugawa family over all Japan. The emperor had become a figurehead.

But when Commodore Matthew C. Perry of the U. S. Navy appeared at Uraga in 1853 with his black gunboats, Japanese society, which had been preserved as still as a bee in amber for 250 years, was set in the most violent internal commotion. Faced with America's military might, Ii Nao-suke, chief minister of the Tokugawa *shogun*, finally took it on himself to abandon the exclusion policy and conclude a commercial treaty with the United States.

This triggered immediate opposition even within the Tokugawa *shogunate*. Rekko, the *daimyo* of Mito, himself vice-*shogun*, spearheaded the attack against opening the country to outsiders. His party followed the principle of *sonno-joi*, "restore the emperor's rule and drive out the foreigners."

"When the then *shogun* died young," Matsuda-san explains, "naturally the suspicion fell on Rekko, the Lord of Mito. And as Rekisenin Oka was his favorite physician, suspicion focused on him as having poisoned the *shogun*.

"As a result, Rekisenin Oka was sentenced to death. He was ordered to commit *harakiri*, an honorable form of suicide that demands the utmost in personal fortitude, requiring a samurai to disembowel himself with his own short sword.

"Too late, his name was cleared. But Lord Rekko of Mito sympathized with his widow and gave her a pension of rice for the rest of her life."

Oka's death was a great blow to his family. But it could not keep good fortune from Matsuda-san's grandfather.

"The very fact that he was the adopted son of the noted physician of the powerful lord of Mito won for him the chance to study at Nagasaki," Matsuda-san explains.

"Grandfather used a Dutch-Japanese dictionary. I still remember the copies my grandfather made from the original with a writing brush and ink on very thin sheets of paper made from the wood pulp of a certain tree. My sister also told me she remembered an anatomical chart of twins in the womb drawn by our grandfather himself."

19

One thing puzzles Matsuda-san to this day.

"I can't quite understand why my exceptional grandfather, one of the very few progressive physicians of his time, came to be the bridegroom of the only daughter of an obscure country doctor in such an out-of-the-way place."

The problem was compounded by an unusual marriage arrangement. Matsuda-san's grandmother was an only child. Since the Orient attaches great importance to the persistence of the family and its name, Japan has developed an ingenious system for preserving it. A husband for the only child is adopted into the family. He becomes a *muko-yoshi*, an adopted bridegroom. The bride, in this case, is called a *mukotorimusume*, a daughter who takes a bridegroom into her own house.

The bride kept her family name, Satoko Okawa. And the young physician now became Dr. Okawa. For the second time in his life he became adopted. Previously he had been known as Oka, after Rekisenin Oka, who had adopted him as a boy. Now his surname was lengthened a bit as he became Okawa. But the meaning had changed completely. Oka means "hill," while Okawa signifies "great river." To become an adopted bridegroom and surrender one's surname requires no small sacrifice in a country where masculinity has been boldly asserted for 1,500 years. It was particularly galling to a professional man who had already achieved much in his own right.

The situation was ready-made for conflict. And it was not long in coming. Father-in-law and son-in-law were worlds apart. One was conservative, the other progressive. They had been trained in two very different types of medicine, Chinese and Western.

The shadow of misunderstanding and the strain of tension invaded the quiet home of the country doctor. A malady had developed in the household that neither of the doctors, with all their medical skills, could heal. A gulf much wider than a mere generation gap had opened up between them.

"My grandfather finally made up his mind to leave home for good."

It was the beginning of the new and exciting Meiji era. A man of parts could not be content to remain in a sleepy provincial town where his talents were not appreciated.

Now the young wife was torn between her duty toward her conservative father on the one side and her love for her progressive young husband on the other.

"Grandfather urged his wife to follow him, but Grandmother, like most of the women of her day, was too conservative."

Confucian commandments of obedience to parents combined with strong Japanese family feelings to keep her rooted to her ancestral home. Besides, some of the ways of her educated spouse must have seemed strange to one reared in such a provincial and sheltered environment.

Normally, the bride moves into the home of the groom, especially if he is the eldest son. Then this problem might not have arisen. But the bridegroom was adopted. And therefore he had to take up his abode in his wife's ancestral home. And because she was a *mukotorimusume* she felt uniquely compelled to remain and carry on the family and its name. For had her husband not taken her name?

When the brilliant young doctor saw how hard it was for his young wife to tear herself away from her home and her aged parents, he gave her a manuscript he had written on the subject of vaccination.

"If you ever find yourself in a financial fix," he said, "have this published. I am sure it will bring you enough to take care of your family and yourself."

Matsuda-san reflects with a strain of melancholy: "Mother was only a tiny baby when her father parted from her. But then and there tragedy entered her life. Many things might have been different for her."

But Matsuda-san does not think hard thoughts about her grandmother. She finds much to admire in her and loves to talk about her.

"My grandmother came out of the time when Japan was still asleep under *sakoku,* her arrogant isolation policy. A great many people, including men and especially women, were left illiterate in those days. 'Women and children are creatures unteachable,' says an old Japanese proverb. Japan's present literacy rate of more than 98 percent is very different from those days.

"At that time, my grandmother was a marvel in the community. Not only could she read and write Japanese, but she was well versed in the highly respected Chinese classics."

Matsuda-san recognizes her debt to her grandmother. There was great strength in the tradition of poise and composure that her grandmother transmitted. Feudalism had great weaknesses but also significant cultural values. The province where Kiyoko-san was born and brought up was one of the most conservative in all Japan. The feudal lord of that province played an important role in the Meiji Restoration. Ardently, he upheld the twin policies of *sonno-joi.* He wanted to honor the emperor and expel the foreigners.

"Grandmother Okawa was born of a proud samurai family. But right after her birth she was adopted by an aunt who had no children. This foster mother, when young, had served as a lady-in-waiting in the inner palace of the Tokugawa shogunate, the military family who had ruled the country in place of the emperor for 250 years. She was well versed, therefore, in Japanese etiquette and was regarded as an accomplished lady. My grandmother was brought up under her strict discipline and was always told that the daughter of a samurai should never lightly show her feelings before others."

She obviously learned her lesson well. Koyoko-san tells about an episode that demonstrates her grandmother's poise and presence of mind.

"One day she was lying on the straw-matted *tatami* floor next to her baby daughter, who became my mother, singing a lullaby to put her to sleep.

"Suddenly a *ronin*, a masterless samurai, brandishing a blood-stained sword, broke into the peaceful room where she lay with her baby."

The agitated *ronin* had burst in still wearing his footgear, something that Japanese otherwise never do. They take off their shoes in the *genkan*, or vestibule, to protect the *tatami* floor matting.

"In a rough voice the *ronin* demanded, 'Where are you hiding the enemy *ronin*?' "

Though the Meiji Restoration had come into effect, many were still dissatisfied with the policy their feudal lord had followed. Those were turbulent days.

"My grandmother then calmly answered without even turning her head, 'How should I know whether someone has come into my house or not when I have been here with my baby the whole time? I haven't been away from her for even an instant. If you care, you can search everywhere inside our house or outside in the garden just as much as you like. I've got nothing to do with your rival *ronin*.'

"And then she went on calmly singing her lullaby to her baby.

"The intruder, on the other hand, was taken aback by my grandmother's composure and went away without another word."

To understand the mortal danger in which Grandmother Okawa found herself, it is helpful to know that the Tokugawa shogunate and the local lords were almighty and that their samurai, too, had the power of life and death over the people. They could do whatever they liked to them. Matsuda-san asked one day,

"Have you heard of the word *tsujigiri?* It means, literally, 'wayside slash.' When a samurai wanted to test his swordsmanship, or when he had obtained a noble new sword, say one created by a famous swordsmith like Masamune, he might go out in the dark of the night with masked face, lie in wait in the shadows of the street, try his new sword on a chance wayfarer, and kill him without any feeling of shame or regret. The samurai simply took this for granted as a privilege of their rank.

"They thought the samurai could do anything to people of the other three classes. If a person did or said anything a samurai found disagreeable, he would just kill him. Those were the days when the lives of the common people were at the mercy of the samurai.

"So you can well understand," Matsuda-san continued, "though the feudal system had been legally abolished, what critical danger threatened my grandmother when the *ronin* ran into her house with his dirty straw sandals still on his feet, waving his bloodstained sword. It was her composure alone that saved my grandmother and her baby daughter, who was to become my mother."

Matsuda-san appreciates the good points of her traditional culture.

This was one occasion when Grandmother Okawa's strict Confucian upbringing stood her in good stead. Her foster mother had always told her that it is a shame to show one's feelings easily before others. This characterized her attitude all her life.

Matsuda-san does recall one great exception.

"The only time I ever saw her lose her temper was when I told her that I should like to become a Christian."

Kiyoko-san tells another tale of her grandmother's unfailing self-possession.

"One night Grandmother suddenly felt acute pain in her left eye. In the morning she asked my mother to hire a *rikisha,* a 'man-pulled cart,' a vehicle that had first been invented by a Western missionary for his invalid wife, to take her to an eye surgeon in the city about 20 kilometers away to undergo an immediate operation. That was before railroads and buses came to our quiet countryside.

"It was acute glaucoma. When Grandmother came home from the hospital, she told us that if she had not had prompt surgery she might have lost the sight of the other eye as well.

"You see, she was the wife of a doctor. Because she knew something about the disease, she could make the right decision. She never missed the mark."

Matsuda-san recalls the shingle that her grandfather had hung out. On this wooden signboard was the picture of a human eye, advertising that her grandfather was an eye doctor as well as a surgeon and general practitioner. But what particularly impressed Matsuda-san was her grandmother's quiet composure.

"After she came home she said little about her sudden operation. She went on doing her household chores as usual, even the sewing of which she was so fond. Except for the members of our family no one in the neighborhood knew that she had lost the sight of her left eye. She always told us that when one is ill one should not make life unpleasant and unhappy for others by grumbling and complaining about it."

Matsuda-san's grandmother, like most Japanese, Christians and non-Christians alike, was greatly attracted to Christian hymns. Grandmother had a good ear for poetry herself. Kiyoko-san remembers, "My grandmother was very clever in composing Japanese poems. She wrote one right after baptism, expressing her joy at being saved by the grace of God."

Both her acquired Christian faith and the strong samurai ideals inherited from her ancestors were valuable gifts to an appreciative granddaughter. Together, they made an invincible combination. Together they gave power to her Christian witness in the times of severest trial. The good gifts that come from the Creator and those she received from the Redeemer and the Holy Spirit did not oppose each other.

Her grandmother's teaching not to bother other people by complaining about one's own pain and misery led Matsuda-san, quite unwittingly, to introduce a young relative to Christianity. Even after she had already lost her jawbone, God used her in an astonishing way to win people to Christ.

Full many a gem of purest ray serene

   The dark unfathomed caves of ocean bear:

Full many a flower is born to blush unseen,

   And waste its fragrance on the desert air.

   — *Elegy Written in a Country Churchyard*
   Thomas Gray (1716 — 1771)

CHAPTER THREE

Mother: A Gem Unseen

It was 1870, the third year of the Meiji era, when Kiyoko's mother was born. She was one of the few girls to be admitted to the elementary school system then being established for the first time.

So quick and bright was she in her studies that the teachers allowed her to enter the third grade, skipping the first two grades entirely. Later she was awarded a prize by the prefectural governor for her outstanding scholastic performance.

"Mother was, of course, very eager to continue her studies, but she was not allowed to do so, simply because she was the only daughter in the family. Instead, she had to marry my father," Matsuda-san recounts in words familiar to many unhappy Japanese women.

"He was not Mother's choice. Grandmother had selected him. And Mother became another poor victim of the family system!"

Again, an unusual marriage had been arranged. For once more, the Okawa household was faced with the need of adopting a bridegroom to carry on the family and the name. The history of the previous generation was repeating itself.

Bereft of her husband, Grandmother Satoko Okawa had

endured a very hard time sustaining her family. Both of her aged parents had suffered strokes and had become bedridden. And for years her fatherless little girl had been too young to be of any help.

Grandmother Okawa was naturally afraid to risk her daughter's future and her own by selecting another brilliant, spirited bridegroom like her own *mukoyoshi* had been. She sought one better suited to the role.

"My father was a good man, but he had little in common with Mother. She always yearned for more knowledge and progress."

Matsuda-san's mother was very different from her grandmother. And looking back, Kiyoko understands her motivation as well.

"Because of her father's rare accomplishments as a doctor, and because of her own unfulfilled desire for study, Mother made up her mind when I was born that I should receive the highest education available for girls in those early years of the Meiji era."

When Kiyoko finished the six years of primary school in 1903 at 12 years of age, her mother had her take the entrance examination at the new Girls High School, which had opened only a few years earlier at Mito. It was the only girls high school in the entire prefecture.

In those days the aim of girls' education in high school was to prepare them to be "good wives and wise mothers." In line with that thinking, the curriculum paid scant attention to the study of the English language. It was merely an elective subject. Many of Kiyoko's classmates chose to take additional sewing and handicraft lessons instead of English. She was strongly tempted to follow the same path of least resistance.

"I was from a small primary school in the country. And when the first English lesson was given, I found to my dismay that most of the girls from the city schools already knew the alphabet. Since I was so far behind, I feared that I would never be able to keep up with them. So I made up my mind to give up the study of English for more fascinating subjects like sewing and handicraft."

When Kiyoko-san told her mother that she had resolved to give up English, she had no doubt that her parent would consent at once. But she had misjudged her mother.

"No!"

Japanese women look dainty and fragile. They appear to be pliable and soft. But there is more steel in them than their appearance would suggest.

Sternly, the mother frowned at her 12-year-old Kiyoko-san.

"All right! If you are giving up the study of English, you might as well quit school altogether."

Little Kiyoko-san was taken aback.

"I was not at all prepared to receive such a severe rebuff from my mother. I was at a loss what to do. To leave the school I had so eagerly wished to enter was of course out of the question. Very reluctantly, I told Mother that I would continue the study of English."

Her mother at once softened her voice and promised to do what she could to help her out of her frustrating situation. She added, "Have I told you the story of Helen Keller? She can neither see nor hear. And yet she managed to complete a college education."

Among Japanese who met Helen Keller was Miss Utako Shimoda, who laid the foundations for Jissen Women's College in Shibuya, Tokyo, on the threshold of the 20th century in 1899. Prior to that she served as lady-in-waiting to the empress. She was so clever in composing poetry that the empress told her to change her name to Utako. "Uta" means poem. For the rest of her life she was known as "maker of songs." At her encounter with Helen Keller, Miss Shimoda casually asked, "Do you speak French?"

Miss Keller was ready for the challenge. At once she placed her fingers on Miss Shimoda's lips and urged her to speak to her in French. But Miss Shimoda was plunged into embarrassment and shame. For she herself could not speak French, while the internationally famous blind and deaf girl was quite prepared to understand the language even through the tips of her fingers.

After telling Kiyoko-san this story, her mother continued, "You have complete use of your five senses. Why should you think of giving up the study of but a single foreign language? You remember your grandfather's Dutch dictionary, don't you? He had to copy it from the original with a writing brush and India ink. You have good teachers to help you. You have good dictionaries to consult. Why don't you make a good try?"

It was her mother who infused into 12-year-old Kiyoko-san some of the iron of her own determination.

" 'Think of Miss Keller!'

"That was my mother's favorite word whenever she encouraged us to overcome difficulties confronting us.

"It really was amazing that Mother should have known the name of Helen Keller in those early days of the twentieth century. When I asked my classmates, not even those who came from city schools had the faintest idea of who and what Miss Keller was."

Why did Helen Keller make an unforgettable impact on Kiyoko-san's mother and on her? No doubt there were many factors, but one reason surely lay in this: Helen Keller's courageous conquest of enormous obstacles suited the family's traditional samurai ideals of fighting and overcoming impossible odds. Japanese people do not simply imitate. They have a genius for adopting and adapting items from abroad that strengthen their age-old cultural values.

Kiyoko-san's mother played the role of educator for her family.

"My mother's desire for self-education could not be quenched in spite of her difficult situation as wife and mother of several children living in a home without any modern conveniences. I found out later that she had subscribed to *Jogaku Zasshi,* a women's study magazine published from 1885 to 1904 by the Meiji Girls' School, one of the first women's colleges in Japan. The school was operated by very progressive teachers, most of whom were Christians. It was a very edifying magazine, entirely different from those being published nowadays for women. For instance, the translation of *Little Lord Fauntleroy,* so much loved and so widely read by our children, first appeared in this magazine. The translator, another outstanding staff member of Meiji Girls' School, was Mrs. Kashi Iwamoto, who used the pen name Shizuko Wakamatsu. She was one of the outstanding Christian women of the Meiji era. Her aim in translating English books into Japanese was to spread and cultivate Christian thought through literature."

Mrs. Iwamoto was born in 1863 of a samurai family of Wakamatsu in north central Japan. Like many other samurai, her father was impoverished by the end of the feudal age in the Meiji Restoration of imperial rule. No longer did they receive handsome allowances of rice from their *daimyo.* Kashi's parents were so poverty-stricken that at the age of seven she was given away to a merchant of Yokohama, who happened to be visiting in her town at the time. Personally, she was plunged into deep depression by the trauma of being given away by her own father and mother. Socially, this was a great comedown for Kashi, as merchants had been in the fourth and lowest social class, while the samurai had been in the top layer. But this cruel step was God's plan to make her

32

life count for Him, just as He permitted Joseph to be sold into Egypt. The merchant at once placed Kashi into Ferris Seminary, opened just then in 1870 by the Reformed Church in America. And thus she became the very first graduate of the first Protestant mission school in Japan.

Though Kashi Iwamoto never went abroad, her command of English was so easy and perfect that she regularly contributed to a number of American magazines. She was one of those bridge persons who interpreted the best of America and England to Japan and vice versa. Like her merchant foster father, she learned to barter, but in cultural and spiritual goods. She lived at Meiji Girls' School in Tokyo, which she managed with her husband. Unfortunately, she died tragically in 1895 at only 33 when her home was destroyed by fire. But not before she had provided people like Matsuda-san's mother with much good reading material.

Neither Matsuda-san's mother nor her grandmother were Christians at this time. Nor was she herself. But Christian literature was beginning to reach them and make its impact on them.

Japanese readers appreciated Kashi Iwamoto's translation of *Little Lord Fauntleroy* perhaps because of the stress Frances Eliza Hogdson's story lays on good manners. Unfamiliar to this generation, the tale centers on Cedric Errol, who comes to England at the age of seven with his American mother upon becoming heir to his grandfather, an earl. Beautifully bred in both character and manners, he wins the affection of his crusty old grandfather. After defeating a pretender to the estate, he reconciles his grandfather with his mother.

Akatsuki no tsurube ni agaru

tsubaki kana

Dawnlight, and from the well

up comes the bucket — in it

a camellia bell.

—Kakei (1648 — 1716)

CHAPTER FOUR

Off to College in Tokyo

Nine-year-old Kiyoko-san, shining black hair tied in braids, took off her *geta,* the wooden clogs she used for street wear, in the *genkan,* front hall of the home where she lived with her mother and grandmother.

"*Tadaima!*" "I'm here now," she called in well-bred greeting.

"*Okaerinasai!*" "Welcome home!" came her mother's cheerful and traditional response.

Hardly had the young fourth-grader entered the *tatami* straw-matted living room when her mother showed her a picture of two girls in the newspaper.

"Look at these girls, Kiyoko-chan! They are going abroad to continue their education."

Drawing close for a better look, Kiyoko-san saw two girls, one sitting and the other standing.

"The government is sending these two graduates of the Tokyo Girls' Higher Teachers' School to America."

The two girls, one named Miss Okada and the other Miss Okonogi, later Mrs. Tsuji, upon their return became professors of their alma mater, presently known as Ocha-nomizu Women's University, supported by the national government.

36

That picture made an unforgettable impression on little Kiyoko. In ways like this her mother nourished the flame of ambition and determination in her daughter. The dream of overseas study was planted into little Kiyoko's heart. And the intelligent little girl was to come close indeed to realizing that dream. As a matter of fact, she was to spend time abroad with her professor husband one day.

Kiyoko-san's alert mother, eager for her daughter to have the opportunities that had been denied her, left no stone unturned. At 80 years of age Matsuda still gratefully remembers: "When I was about to graduate from high school in 1907 at the age of sixteen, it was mother who told me to apply for the entrance examinations at Tsuda College in Tokyo.

"I still don't know how she found out about Tsuda College, which had been founded only seven years earlier in 1900 as Joshi Eigaku Juku, Women's English School. Umeko Tsuda had given up teaching at the Peeress' School because she felt that the nation needed a school for thoroughly prepared teachers, primarily for instructors in English. Only ten students were enrolled in her new school at its precarious start. Even in 1907 when I entered, it was a very small and modest private school with an enrollment of less than a hundred. Now, of course, it enjoys the reputation of being one of the best women's colleges in the country."

Today, especially their top-level command of the English language distinguishes Tsuda College graduates. The present campus in Kodaira, a city of suburban Tokyo, is a mecca for girls who wish to excel in English and mathematics. Tsuda graduates are eagerly sought after, particularly as teachers of English and as interpreters and translators.

But when sixteen-year-old Kiyoko-san took her entrance examination and was one of the fortunate few to be admitted, Tsuda College bore a disappointing exterior. The unimpressive structures were incongruously out of character with the considerable reputation the college had acquired then already. There were but a few wooden classroom buildings. Chairs with writing arms shaped like tennis rackets served as desks.

The school was centrally located in Tokyo at Gobancho in Kojimachi, right behind the British embassy, which fronts on the outer moat of the emperor's palace.

Nostalgia carries Matsuda-san back to her happy college days.

"We students were drawn to the promenade in front of the embassy. It was one of our favorite places, especially in early April when the *sakura* were blooming in Tokyo.

"A double line of flowering cherry trees flanked the road between the embassy and the promenade.

"How gaily we college girls laughed and talked under the cherry trees as we enjoyed our walks there, after the day's work in school was over!"

Though the blossom petals fell from the trees long ago, and though the days of her youth whirled away in the winds of time, Matsuda-san remembers both as though it were yesterday.

The cherry trees still bloom each April in Gobancho. But the halls of Tsuda College, hung with memories dear to the heart of Matsuda-san, no longer exist.

In the Great Earthquake of 1923 Tsuda College was completely destroyed by fire. That disaster cost 100,000 lives. Great sections of Yokohama and Tokyo were devastated. The quake struck just before noon when millions of housewives were preparing the midday meal over small *hibachi,* clay charcoal-burning stoves, which have now been adopted by many American backyard barbecue artists. These *hibachi* were overturned by the tremors. Countless fires soon were licking at the flimsy wood, straw, and paper of Japanese dwellings. In one congested area tens of thousands were suffocated when the raging sea of flames devoured all the oxygen. A monument has been erected to those poor victims. Tokyo had never known such fire storms before. They were a grim presentiment of what was to come in the fire bombings of World War II. Damage wrought by the Great Earthquake extended out into the entire Kanto area, which includes not only Tokyo but the five surrounding prefectures.

But Kiyoko-san as a first-year student at Tsuda did not even dream of such future horrors.

"Fresh from a school in a provincial town, I found college completely new and entrancing."

At Mito she had attended an old-style four-year junior high school of the type established long before the present school reforms were put into effect during the American Occupation after World War II.

The new freshman from the country noticed a big difference between her high school and the college she now attended in the heart of the capital.

"In junior high school everything had been rigidly regulated by mere rules. Mutual understanding between teachers and students did not exist.

"But at Tsuda the number of students admitted was carefully limited. Naturally, teachers and students came to know one another very well. Particularly we boarding students were on close terms with the faculty."

Umeko Tsuda, founder and first president of Tsuda College, was one of five girls sent abroad by the government to study at the beginning of the Meiji era. This was the first time Japanese girls were given such an opportunity. They formed a distinguished delegation. One of the five later married Prince Oyama, commander in chief of the Japanese army. Another became the wife of Rear Admiral Uryu, a graduate of the U. S. Naval Academy at Annapolis, and gained the title of baroness. Umeko was the youngest in the quintet, being only six years of age. One's heart goes out to a little girl so young having to leave mother and father and study far away across the sea in a land filled with long-nosed foreigners speaking a strange tongue.

Her father, Sen Tsuda, must have been a remarkable man. As an authority on agriculture he knew that Japan was far behind in this area when compared with many foreign countries. He was always pushing for progress.

Matsuda-san cites the story of "Mr. Tsuda and the Tomato." In the nineteenth century tomatoes were not universally appreciated even in the West. Some horticulturists regarded them as purely decorative plants. In Europe they were called "love apples" because they were suspected of having aphrodisiac powers. Many uneducated people thought they were poisonous or, at any rate, not good to eat.

"In those days," Matsuda-san recounts, "tomatoes were called 'red egg plants' by the Japanese, and almost nobody cared to eat them."

But some farmers near Yokohama had planted tomatoes in their fields to meet the demand by foreigners who lived in the nearby port city.

One day Sen Tsuda came bowling along in a *rikisha* on his way to Tokyo. He spotted those tomatoes. At once he ordered the *rikisha* to stop.

"Most Japanese didn't like the peculiar flavor. But Mr. Tsuda enjoyed tomatoes so very much that he got down from his *rikisha*, stalked out into the field in his good clothing, picked the tomatoes right from the vines, and ate them on the spot. To say that his *rikisha* puller was astonished is to put it mildly."

Matsuda-san has it right when she declares, "It was

because Tsuda-san was such a progressive man that he could make up his mind to send his six-year-old daughter Umeko to a faraway country like America."

Eleven long years with a model family in America left their profound impact on the plastic mind of the child.

"When she returned to Japan as a young woman, she had entirely forgotten the Japanese language. Her father had to interpret for her. Though she was born a Japanese, her way of thinking had become entirely American."

Later she went to America a second time and attended Bryn Mawr, one of the country's topflight women's colleges.

But Umeko tried hard to become as Japanese as possible.

"During the five years I spent at Tsuda College," Matsuda-san remembers, "I did not see her wear a foreign dress even once. She always appeared in Japanese kimono."

To the students she was now known by that beloved and respectful title of *sensei*, teacher. As a samurai respects and serves his *daimyo,* so a Japanese student in older, more intimate times before mass education reached the college level, respected every one of his *sensei.* But he would choose one in particular to love and serve and consult on every important issue of his life, including the choice of an occupation or a marriage partner. Tsuda-sensei was highly respected by the students, especially because she was also the *kocho-sensei,* the president of the college.

Just as she herself strove to be a true Japanese woman, so Tsuda-sensei wanted to make sure that her charges would not lose their lovely Japanese femininity and their capacity to be good wives and mothers.

"As it was, outsiders tended to look on us English students as shockingly progressive.

"Tsuda-sensei did not want us to become pedantic and undomestic bluestockings. She abhorred the very thought."

In order to make sure that they would become good,

well-trained wives, she hired a Japanese sewing teacher for the boarding students until they became seniors.

But Kiyoko-san had come a long way since her high school days when she had tried in vain to give up English in favor of sewing.

"To be truthful, most of us didn't like those sewing lessons."

But Tsuda-sensei did not let matters rest with sewing.

"She also made sure that we became well accustomed to things around the kitchen.

"She had us boarders, five or six at a time, take turns preparing dinner each Saturday evening. We would always invite the teachers, both Japanese and foreign. And when she could spare the time, Miss Tsuda herself came to partake of our frugal dinner."

Sometimes the students would invite a distinguished guest from outside the school.

"It was to one of these evening parties, the farewell dinner for my graduating class, that we invited the famous Dr. Inazo Nitobe."

Dr. Nitobe later became a secretary of the League of Nations at Geneva, long before the United Nations was headquartered in New York.

His main concern was to establish mutual understanding and cordial friendship among all nations, especially between Japan and America. His famous last words, breathed just before he died in Victoria, Canada, on his ninth and last visit to North America in 1933, were:

"How I wish I could be a bridge spanning the Pacific to connect Japan and America!"

He himself had entered into an international marriage. His wife was an American lady whose family were devoted members of the Society of Friends.

"While her Quaker brother was alive," Kiyoko-san

relates, "it was his custom to send each of us Tsuda College students a copy of the English Bible from America as a graduation gift."

Matsuda-san has never forgotten that farewell evening dinner party shortly before her graduation.

"It was then that Dr. Nitobe uttered those memorable words which became etched in my mind and served as the guiding principle of my life."

Standing to address what was perhaps the best educated group of young women in the nation, he said to them with great earnestness:

"Girls, now that you have finished your entire course of study and are about to embark on the wide, wide ocean of the world, you might think of yourselves as full-fledged English scholars.

"But no! You have only been given a key to open the inexhaustibly rich civilization of the Western world. And it's entirely up to you whether you make use of the key with which you have been endowed. You see, studying is a lifelong work. If you stop studying, you will be rolling back to a status lower than you have now.

"So, girls, keep on studying!"

More than half a century later Matsuda-san was still recalling — and following! — the advice of one of Japan's most distinguished scholars and statesmen.

"These words of Dr. Nitobe were so deeply engraved on my memory that I always felt the urge to continue studying in whatever circumstances I found myself.

"That was why I began to study German at 77 and Russian at 79. Of course, foreign languages are not the only challenge. Various kinds of study invite us. But for me, a simple old woman like me, studying foreign languages is a joy.

"I never tire of studying anything new. For example,

when I began to learn German, my main object was to understand German well enough to read Theodor Storm's *Im-
mensee*. In this story an old man's thoughts turn to his
childhood sweetheart, who had been for him like a beautiful
water flower beyond his reach. But now my interest in German is no longer limited to such a narrow groove.

"I simply enjoy studying."

Ikuhiro mo

kyo yori nobiyo,

hime komatsu!

Itoshinaki yo no

ne o katamete.

Like a sapling pine,

Keep on growing fathoms more,

Princess, than today.

In a world that pities not

Sink your roots, make them strong!

—Satoko Okawa

CHAPTER FIVE

Fun and Work at Tsuda College

Life was not all serious work at Tsuda College. Matsuda-san recalls, "After our Saturday evening dinners we spent a few happy hours with our faculty guests, including sometimes even Miss Tsuda. We played games, did folk dances, and the like.

"The game we played most often was a word game in which we would complete a sentence with an adjective. For example: 'Mrs. Gardiner's cat is _____.' We would think up an adjective to put into the blank space, like this: 'Mrs. Gardiner's cat is amiable.' Each student in turn would change the adjective. When we seemed to have exhausted the adjectives beginning with the letter 'a,' we would proceed to 'b.' Sometimes the adjectives used were very funny, absurd, or even illogical, but so long as they were adjectives, they were allowed to pass. I think this helped a great deal to enlarge our vocabulary.

"Then, before the party broke up, we usually sang together a pleasant little song which one of the faculty, Miss Anna C. Hartshorne, had written for us. It went like this:

> When we first came to Gobancho,
>> Preps were we as green as grass.

Now as sober English students,
     Smile we o'er the verdant past.
Refrain:

Joshi Eigakujuku, Joshi Eigaku ni,
     At Gobancho Kojimachi,
We speak English every day.

There we learn pronunciation.
     There we study Attic lore.
There with grammar and with spelling
     We perplex our heads full sore.
Refrain

The alumnae all remind us
     We must keep our tenses right,
And departing leave behind us
     Reputations just as bright.
Refrain

Like young students everywhere, the girls at Tsuda took roguish delight in their superior knowledge of a foreign tongue. This was long before the days of the women's liberation movement. In Japanese society the Confucian ethical code made the husband supreme in every sense. To wife and children his word was law. Perhaps it was for this reason that Miss Tsuda's English students took a perverse pleasure in helping a male make himself ridiculous. At any rate, it added another word to Kiyoko-san's rapidly growing vocabulary. Best of all, she could understand an "in" joke at her new school.

"When I first moved into the dormitory, I often heard the word *henpecked* spoken by the senior boarders when they went out shopping. One day a senior boarder asked,

" 'Do you have any shopping to do? Would you like to come along with me to the henpecked?'

"As a new student I was only too happy to accompany a girl from the topmost class.

"When we arrived at a grocery shop near our college, she announced,

" 'Here we are at the henpecked.'

"So I came to understand that *henpecked* meant a grocery shop. I asked her, 'Does *henpecked* mean a grocery shop?'

"She just laughed and wrote down the word for me on a piece of paper, saying, 'You had better find out for yourself what it means.'

"When we got back, I at once consulted the dictionary; there I read, with growing confusion, this definition of the verb *henpeck:* 'to domineer over; worry or harass by ill temper and petty annoyances; nag: said of a wife who thus controls her husband.'

"I was all the more puzzled.

"But gradually I came to understand why the seniors had given the nickname to the shop.

"The owner of the shop must have thought that *henpecked* was a nice English word for a grocery shop. And he seemed rather proud of the nickname and of his mastery of an English word.

"So when he came to our dormitory to solicit grocery orders, he would simply call out in a loud voice,

" '*Tadaima!* Here I am! Henpecked! Do you have any orders for me?'

"Whenever I heard him speak this way, it was hard for me to keep from laughing," Matsuda-san remembers with a degree of mischief even today.

But serious work abounded in Matsuda-san's college days.

"Miss Tsuda was a marvelous teacher. Even though she was the president, she taught the entering class of students. She taught us translation in our freshman year by using

Emile Souvestre's *The Attic Philosopher in Paris: Or, a Peep at the World from a Garret, Being the Journal of a Happy Man.* This was one of my very favorite books. She used it over and over again with the freshman classes for more than ten successive years.

"Nor was she concerned simply about the translation lessons. Rather, she hoped this book would engrave on our minds what real happiness is and how we might find it.

"For example, in the first chapter of the book, the author compares two families, one rich and the other poor.

"A satiated rich man's wife fares forth in her new carriage drawn by thoroughbred horses to distribute her New Year's gifts.

"On the other hand, a poor old woman who made bandboxes for a living enjoyed a frugal but heartwarming party with her three orphaned grandchildren. The 'attic philosopher' who had arranged it, observed,

" 'I had brought only the supper. The bandboxmaker and her children supplied the enjoyment.'

"The evening passed like a moment. The poor philosopher discovered that no one is so unhappy as to have nothing to give and nothing to receive.

"As the philosopher slowly came home, he met his rich neighbor's equipage. She too had just returned from her evening's party; and as she sprang from the carriage step with feverish impatience, he heard her murmur,

" 'At last!'

"But the philosopher when reluctantly leaving the bandboxmaker's joyous family, had said,

" 'So soon!'

"In this we were led to understand the meaning of these two expressions, 'At last!' and 'So soon!'

"More important, Miss Tsuda thereby taught us what real happiness is."

Umeko Tsuda imparted to her students a high level of competence in English. But she did much more.

"Another of Miss Tsuda's favorites was 'Enoch Arden' by Alfred Lord Tennyson. A shipwrecked sailor returns after long years as a solitary castaway to find that he has been given up for dead. His wife is happily remarried and now has borne a child by her new husband, who is also providing well for Enoch's children. Through the window he sees the warmth, the peace, the happiness of the family, and he wrenches himself away without revealing himself.

"By means of this poem Miss Tsuda showed us Enoch's noble spirit of self-denial. Without her explanations we would never have understood the depth of agony expressed in his prayer.

> Too hard to bear! why did they take me thence?
> O God Almighty, blessed Saviour, Thou
> That didst uphold me on my lonely isle,
> Uphold me, Father, in my loneliness
> A little longer! aid me, give me strength
> Not to tell her, never to let her know.
> Help me not to break in upon her peace.
> My children too! must I not speak to these?
> Never, no father's kiss for me—the girl
> So like her mother, and the boy, my son.

"In this way we were not only taught English, but an ever higher and nobler Christian love was planted in our mind, opening new vistas for our future lives.

"Here is another example that shows how clever she was in illuminating literary classics that seemed to us almost incomprehensible. When we were trying to read Robert Browning's 'Andrea Del Sarto,' we found it so difficult that we could make neither head nor tail of it.

"Then she began to read in her low, mellow, smooth voice the lines,

> A common grayness silvers everything —
> . . . .
> Ah, but a man's reach should exceed his grasp,
> Or what's a heaven for? All is silver-gray,
> Placid and perfect with my art: the worse!

"With consummate skill she communicated both the evening scene and the poet's intent. In one vivid flashing insight she made us understand that the technical perfection which had earned for Andrea Del Sarto the title of 'The Faultless Painter' was both his glory and despair. Like his beautiful mistress, his art lacked soul."

Later, Kiyoko-san had the rare privilege of being admitted as a special student to Tokyo University, when this number-one school of higher learning in Japan was opened to women students for the first time. Tokyo Daigakko, or "Todai" as it is colloquially known, has played in Japan the kind of exalted role that Harvard, Yale, and Princeton would in the United States, if they were all combined on one campus.

Matsuda-san testifies, "I found none of the lectures at this great university so fascinating as those given by Miss Umeko Tsuda.

"I deem it a great privilege that I was admitted to such a fine school as Tsuda College at a time when few girls were offered such an opportunity. In return for what I was given in those early years, I feel that I should do something for others less favored."

Opportunity offers pain as well as pleasure. Striving occasions strain. Growth is accompanied by anxiety.

To promote mastery of English Miss Tsuda emphasized the writing of English compositions. In exchange, she excused the upper-class students from one exercise that annoyed most of them, as Matsuda-san recalls.

"When we became seniors we were exempt from the Saturday morning sewing lessons, because we had to spend a great deal of time preparing our English essays.

"It was not simply the English that mattered, but the content as well. Tsuda-sensei would assign such topics as 'Women's Social Status in Japan,' and 'Peace or War?'"

In order to write about such a subject, the student had to read a great many books, do other research, and meditate on the problem. Then came the labor of arranging a logical outline and writing the complete text of the essay.

With fear and trembling the students approached the hour of the class. Anxiously they debated the question, "Who will Miss Tsuda call on to read her essay?"

Once the lot had fallen, the chosen one mustered what courage she could and read her essay aloud. Then began a thoroughgoing dissection of the ideas and opinions the writer had tried to express. Sometimes even the English style was criticized.

"It really was a trial for the writer of the essay. Miss Tsuda was not a lenient teacher. All of us just prayed that we would not be called on to read."

Most of the girls had been reared in a sheltered, domestic setting. In their mothers they had seen the models of domestic femininity with a rather small circle of interest and concern.

Today, newspapers like *Asahi, Yomiuri,* and *Mainichi* boast the largest circulations in the world with many millions of copies daily. It is difficult to imagine that it was not always so. But Matsuda-san reminds us:

"In the latter part of the Meiji era, subscriptions to daily papers were not so common as now. Few families took them.

"For women, reading the papers was thought to be an

extraordinary waste of time. Even those women who perused them mostly limited their interest to sensational accounts of accidents or other human interest stories."

But Tsuda-sensei, who had studied abroad, led her charges into a larger world.

"Miss Tsuda wanted to open our eyes wider, not only to movements inside Japan, but also to tides of change in the whole world. For this purpose she saw to it that one of the teachers led a current-topics period once a week.

"In order to attend this class, we had to prepare ourselves by reading the newspapers thoroughly to search out something worth reporting. It might be in politics, economics, or some other area.

"Then we had to report the news in English to Miss Fanny Green, a veteran professor, who had previously lived in China. If she found that our accounts had not been thoroughgoing, she would comment in further detail. In this way she allowed us to see more clearly what was going on in the world and helped us understand the causes and consequences of events."

Such discussions of contemporary history shaped Kiyoko-san for a lifetime.

"I still remember the name of Sun Yat Sen, the Chinese revolutionist who overturned the Ching Dynasty.

"Unconsciously shaped by such training, I am still much more keenly interested in the political and social affairs of the world at large than in the soap operas and melodramas broadcast or televised every day."

Matsuda-san is generous in her tribute to the dedicated foreign teachers who helped Tsuda-sensei achieve her goals.

"Anna C. Hartshorne was a wonderful Christian. Like Dr. Nitobe, she was an indispensable support to Miss Tsuda."

The latter acquired this lifelong friend and co-worker

in an unusual way. Miss Tsuda's father, ever interested in progress in almost any field, had come across an interesting medical book by a Dr. Charles Hartshorne of Philadelphia and had translated it. When the author heard of this, he paid a visit to Japan. And with him came his daughter Anna. The two were enchanted with the country and prolonged their visit.

"Miss Hartshorne's father loved Japan so much that he wished to be buried in Japanese soil at his death. He now rests peacefully in Tokyo's Aoyama Cemetery," Matsuda-san recalls.

Each spring the petals fall like snow on his grave while the multitudes throng the cemetery to enjoy the famous cherry blossoms of Aoyama.

When Anna Hartshorne met the daughter of the man who translated her father's book, and when she learned about her school, she felt that she had found her life work.

Michi Kawai, who also taught at Tsuda, commented, "The devoted friendship of these two is an example of the great friendship which is possible between people of different races. Miss Hartshorne persistently kept herself in the background. But without her, Miss Tsuda's work would have fallen short of the greatness it attained."

"Miss Hartshorne sought neither fame nor riches," Matsuda-san recalls. "Her only concern was how to help Miss Tsuda and her school. They say she worked without pay. Moreover, she gave everything she had for the school, spending very little for herself."

When the Great Kanto Earthquake of September 1, 1923, completely destroyed the college by the ensuing fire, Miss Hartshorne went to America at once to get help. Together with Mrs. Yone Abiko, Miss Tsuda's younger sister who was living in the U. S. A., she began a fund-raising campaign for the school's rehabilitation that netted half a million dollars. Matsuda-san voices the feelings of other Tsuda graduates when she writes:

"We should always remember Miss Hartshorne with deep gratitude for her self-forgetting efforts on behalf of our school. The Tsuda alumnae rallied to assist her, eagerly helping to rehabilitate their alma mater.

"The funds raised in America and Japan following the disaster enabled the school to buy a large campus in the city of Kodaira located in the Tokyo suburbs. It was then a very quiet place on the Musashi Plain.

"If you will visit there now," Matsuda-san invites, "you will see a well-cared-for campus dotted with beautiful buildings. The lawns are well kept and surrounded with lovely trees. On a clear day, one can see the distant peak of Mount Fuji beyond the mountain ranges."

Tsuda College stands a monument to excellent teachers, to eager students, and to international vision and cooperation.

Love Divine, all love excelling,
  Joy of heav'n, to earth come down,
Fix in us Thy humble dwelling
  All Thy faithful mercies crown.
Jesus, Thou art all compassion,
  Pure, unbounded love Thou art;
Visit us with Thy salvation,
  Enter ev'ry trembling heart.

—Charles Wesley, 1747

CHAPTER SIX

Such Fear — and Such Love

"When I look back over all these years that I have lived, I just can't help feeling that my family and I have been led by some unseen hand," Matsuda-san testifies.

"We grew up in a strict feudalistic atmosphere with strong nationalistic and traditional loyalties in politics and religion."

Her grandmother came out of the Tokugawa period when it was a capital crime to be a Christian. Thousands had been crucified or executed in ways even more cruel. Less than twenty years before Matsuda-san was born, signboards along the highways still offered rewards to anyone who would betray Christians to the authorities. Those signboards were not removed until 1873 when an official Japanese deputation returning from the United States reported that the removal of the antichristian signboards would ease recognition of the new Japanese imperial government by Western powers.

Christianity was a religion both feared and hated. It was enough to make a person's blood run cold to have anyone accuse him of the slightest identification with Christianity. Commodore Perry's famous squadron of "black ships" opened Japan to the outside world by force after 250 years of seclusion.

A Japanese coming aboard one of Perry's ships saw a chaplain drop a prayer book on the deck. Seeing the cross on the cover, the Japanese man's hand involuntarily flew to his throat. The symbol of love divine made him fear for his life.

Matsuda-san reflects on the great odds against entry into the Christian church for herself and her family.

"Don't you think it very strange that in such a setting I dared to go with some of my dormitory friends at the Girls' Junior High School, when I was in my early teens, to see Miss Ada Hannah Wright, an English lady missionary? They say she was born of an aristocratic family.

"I can't recollect exactly how we came to visit Miss Wright. It may have been simply out of curiosity. At any rate, we went to see her in her small *tatami*-floored house attached to the Episcopal Church in the city of Mito, where our high school was."

To this day, Japanese are very hesitant to call at a stranger's house or even to enter a Christian church without an introduction. The courage of those teen-age high school girls is therefore all the more remarkable.

"No one introduced us to her, but she was very glad to see us. It was the first time in my life that I had anything to do with Christian churches and their workers."

It was from Miss Wright that young Kiyoko-san learned her first Christian hymn.

> Jesus loves me. This I know,
> For the Bible tells me so.
> Little ones to Him belong;
> They are weak, but He is strong.

As Kiyoko-san and her schoolmates became better

acquainted with her, Miss Wright told them about her aunt, Miss Hannah Riddell, at Kumamoto City on the large southern island of Kyushyu. Born in London in 1885 and coming to Japan as an independent missionary of the Church of England in 1890, Miss Riddell was the first person to establish a leprosarium in Japan.

"She pioneered this charitable work in the middle of the Meiji era long before our government recognized the need of establishing sanatoriums for leprous patients," Matsuda-san declares in grateful tribute.

The works of love done by Christian missionaries played an important part in dispelling from the minds of the young high school students the strong antipathy against Christianity in which they had been reared.

"Can you imagine what miserable lives these poor lepers led in those days?" Matsuda-san asks. "They were so much detested and abhorred in our country. People believed that leprosy was hereditary. If, unfortunately, someone in the family became infected with the disease, his family would, of course, try to hide him as long as possible. But if the patient became so obviously leprous that he was in danger of discovery, the family would tell the patient to resign himself to his inevitable fate and leave the house in secrecy for the sake of the family.

"Quietly and sorrowfully, the patient would leave the house in the middle of the night, so that no one in the neighborhood would see him.

"For, once known that there was a case of leprosy in the family, no one would marry the sons or daughters of that house.

"The patient was given a little money to sustain himself for the time being. Then he would leave his home forever.

"If he were strong enough to travel, he would walk all the way to Kumamoto. You see, that city was the mecca for leprous patients. They all went to worship Seishoko-sama and pray for healing."

Seishoko-sama was the posthumous name of a famous man who was regarded as having become a Buddha. In the history of Japan he is known as Kiyomasa and was the feudal lord of Kumamoto. It was he who had succeeded in putting down the civil wars among the feudal lords. He had become the commander in chief of the military forces prior to the Tokugawa regime.

But Kiyomasa became infected with leprosy. Tradition says that he was cured of the dread disease by believing in the Nichiren sect of Buddhism. It is from this denomination that the widely known Soka Gakkai with its present emphasis on faith healing is descended.

"Because Seishoko-sama had himself been cured, those who suffered from leprosy believed that if they worshiped him, he would work miracles for them as well," Matsuda-san explains.

"That was why his shrine was always thronged with poor outcast lepers who had begged their way to Kumamoto after exhausting what little money they had been given.

"One lovely spring day, Miss Riddell went sight-seeing at the shrine, perhaps after visiting historic Kumamoto castle. Along the road the cherry trees were in full bloom. Their delicate beauty hung against the blue sky like a white mist. But underneath, countless lepers were begging for alms.

"So deeply moved was Miss Riddell by their miserable plight that she made up her mind then and there to help the poor outcasts. She established a sanatorium for leprous patients to alleviate their misery.

"In order to help support the hospital, they say she even sold all her property in her native England."

The young high school girls were deeply moved by Miss Wright's recital of her aunt's work in Kumamoto. If Christianity is to appeal to Japanese people, it must come to them as a way of life rather than as a speculative system of metaphysics or a jumble of theological formulas. They are profoundly moved by truth when it comes to them in a fascinating personality. And none is more fascinating than Jesus Christ, the Savior of the world.

"We were too young to understand the sources of the ardent love and sympathy that moved Miss Riddell to devote her entire life to those poor wretches," Matsuda-san remembers.

"But we were deeply stirred and made up our minds to save what little money we could out of our allowances and send it to Kumamoto."

Hannah Riddell stands in that long line of women missionaries whose love and faithfulness moves one to wonder and to tears. She lived for her beloved lepers in Kumamoto. And there she died in 1932 at the age of 77. Her obituary says of her:

"She was a true philanthropist and the pioneer in relief work for lepers in Japan. The terrible conditions in which she found them living, neglected and unprotected, led her to devote her life and fortune to their consolation and care. For over 40 years she continued as a faithful servant to these afflicted people.

"The Hospital of the Resurrection of Hope was established with her own funds and with aid she obtained from friends in England and Japan. Her work for the betterment of these afflicted ones brought the situation to the attention of the Government, and her hospital was the first to be recognized by the Imperial Family with a grant of money.

"She is said to have taken care of 1,660 lepers, there being 100 in the hospital at the time of her death. It was also a work international in type as Chinese, Koreans, and Americans have found relief and care within its walls.

"Miss Riddell's work received a great impetus when she was honoured for her work in 1906 by the Emperor, Meiji Tenno, with the decoration of the Order of the Blue Ribbon. Later, in 1924, the Sixth Class Order of the Sacred Treasure was bestowed upon her. At the news of her death the Empress Dowager and the Empress were pleased to honor her with a grant for religious service in view of her long years of relief work for lepers. To her self-sacrificing, devoted love, courage and faithful service is due the present progress of such relief work throughout the land, and also the hope arises that in the future this curse may be exterminated from Japan."

Today that hope has been virtually fulfilled, thanks to pioneers like Hannah Riddell and the niece who bore her middle name.

Ada Hannah Wright, who had first described her aunt's service on behalf of the leprous patients to young Kiyoko Matsuda and her friends, herself took up this work in 1924 at Miss Riddell's request. She became the director of the sanatorium and continued her work for the leprous patients until she died in 1950 after serving in Japan from 1896.

The selfless service of aunt and niece to the people of Japan did not exhaust itself in a brief, dramatic flurry of activity. They poured out their lives over long, monotonous years of obscure toil on behalf of the people of Japan. Both of them died and lie buried in Japan. Such lives have impressed Matsuda-san and other Japanese. The witness of their loving service has changed the minds of many Japanese about the once odious, hated religion of Christianity. People like Hannah Riddell and Ada Wright authenticated Christianity, for they followed in the train of Him who came not to be served but to serve and to give His life a ransom for all.

Such genuine Christians, both foreign and Japanese, touched the life of Kiyoko from her teens to her eighties.

To her, their denominational affiliation was not of primary importance. What mattered was that they were members of the one body of Christ and that they exhibited Him to her. Each contributed priceless gifts to her building up in the faith. Her present spiritual maturity is in the best sense an ecumenical fruit of the Spirit.

Think where man's glory most begins and ends,

And say my glory was I had such friends.

— William Butler Yeats

CHAPTER SEVEN
"I Had Such Friends"

Kiyoko-san was first drawn to Christianity by the loving deeds of those who served Jesus Christ. But she was exposed to the teaching of the verbal Gospel as well, not only by Miss Wright but also at Tsuda College. Yet the influence of teachers and friends of the college was of crucial importance. God does His work in human hearts through the Gospel. But He also works through the living human personalities who carry that Gospel. If Japanese are, indeed, moved by truth embodied in a fascinating personality, then Kiyoko-san was fortunate in being surrounded by the many-splendored gifts that the Creator and the Spirit can give through people.

Yet the communication of the Christian faith was not left to chance human contacts. There is a place for formal, institutional means as well. And Matsuda-san has not forgotten the lifelong good they gave her.

"From Monday to Friday a morning worship service was held before classes began. It was conducted by turns in English and Japanese. On English days Bible readings, hymns, and prayers were all offered in English. The next day everything would be in Japanese. Those English hymns which I still can sing by heart are those I learned at morning chapel.

66

"Of course, our college was not then and is not now a mission school. Those morning services were not compulsory. But all boarders attended, though a few day scholars joined us.

"Sunday was a quiet day free from any school work, and most of us boarders went to church. Some of the girls coming from mission schools were very strict about keeping the Sabbath. They refused to spend any money on Sunday except for the offerings they made at church. We had read about the Puritans of long ago. As we noted how our schoolmates observed the Sabbath, we were reminded of them. Most of us spent the day in quiet rest, writing letters home or to friends."

But the Christian students did more than observe Sunday blue laws. They also shared their faith with the other girls.

"Some of the Christians among the senior boarders opened Bible classes on Sunday afternoon to initiate us non-Christian students into Christianity. Of course, it was not compulsory, but most of us non-Christian boarders were glad to attend."

A long line of outstanding Christian witnesses, both Japanese and foreigners, helped prepare Kiyoko Matsuda for the decisive step of Christian baptism. They came from various nations and sundry denominations. We shall describe them at some length, for they help to explain Matsuda-san. She is a part of all that she has met, especially in the communion of saints. In her old age she wrote:

"Ever since my entry into Tsuda College I had been strongly drawn to Christianity through the kind guidance of those around me, but the person who played the most important role in leading me into the Christian church was Miss Michi Kawai."

In Hokkaido, Michi had become a Christian as a young

girl after her invalid father was converted. Like his ancestors for forty generations, her father had been a priest of the imperial Shinto shrine at Ise, fountainhead of the Shinto cult. At ten years of age she became one of the first group of seven little girls with whom Miss Sarah C. Smith, an American Presbyterian missionary, opened what was later to become one of the leading Christian schools in Japan—Hokusei Jo Gakko (North Star Girls School) in Sapporo. Their next-door neighbors proved to be Dr. Inazo Nitobe and his American wife with their wide interests and vivid personalities. Dr. Nitobe, a remarkable Christian scholar, served at Hokkaido University. When Dr. Nitobe moved south because the climate proved too severe for the health of his American wife, Michi followed them to Tokyo. Through their friendship she was introduced to Miss Umeko Tsuda, recently back from the United States and from Bryn Mawr. She saw to it that Michi Kawai was awarded a scholarship so that she might enjoy the same rare privilege of studying at this fine school. Just at that time, the Nitobes decided to visit America. They invited Michi to accompany them on her way to Bryn Mawr.

There Michi Kawai not only imbibed some of the best education that the West could offer, but she also made many Christian friends who helped deepen her own spiritual experience. During vacations spent at the home of classmates she gained valuable insights into the way Westerners live. This was of great help to her later when she sought to give her own pupils the best that both Eastern and Western homelife had to offer.

Another opportunity of these vacations was the conferences—student conferences, YWCA conferences, conferences of every kind.

Reporting her experiences later, Michi said:

"My narrow ideas were being broadened; I began to

realize that I belonged not only to Japan, but to the world — God's world."

Umeko Tsuda had helped Michi Kawai gain entree to Bryn Mawr. While Michi was in the States, Miss Tsuda started the college that in later years was to bear her name. It was only natural that upon her return Michi Kawai would in turn help Miss Tsuda by accepting a position as a teacher of English and history in the infant college.

But Michi's talents and energy could not be exhausted by just one activity confined to just one college. At this time there arrived in Japan one who was destined to exercise a far-reaching influence on Michi Kawai and on Kiyoko Matsuda — Caroline Macdonald, a graduate of Toronto University and daughter of the speaker of the Canadian House of Commons. She was called to Japan in 1904 at the request of a group of Japanese and foreign women who felt the need of establishing YWCA work among the students who were then flocking into Tokyo in great numbers for higher education.

Michi and Miss Macdonald had met at a YWCA conference in 1902 at Silver Bay, New York. At that time they had hardly expected to encounter one another again in Tokyo. But it was not long before Michi Kawai had been drawn into the work of the "Y" and gradually became the first full-time YWCA secretary in Japan.

In the work of the Y Michi Kawai "followed the gleam," in the words of its famous motto, not only throughout Japan but to many parts of the world, including a brief period as a student at Union Seminary, New York. Her comments on the Student International Conference at Yenching University in Peking were prophetic. They reveal also that no matter how much Japanese people like Michi Kawai or Kiyoko Matsuda are exposed to Western learning they remain tenaciously Japanese.

"The large Chinese delegation spoke far better English than did our Japanese students, yet it seemed to me that many were greatly Westernized at the expense of their own ancient national culture, which seemed a pity.

"We realized something of the tremendous task ahead of the new China when, after having listened to a Chinese scholar speak in English, French, and German with equal fluency, we went outside the college grounds and were suddenly surrounded by a mob of ragged children and deformed beggars. How would they go about bridging the gap between rich and poor, between educated and illiterate?

"That young China was determined on the reconstruction of their ancient country was evident. But impetuosity and selfish purpose in Western civilization would only bring them into confusion. They would have need of endless patience and self-sacrifice."

Later, in the face of great hindrances, Miss Kawai founded another famous girls school, Keisen Jo-Gakuen, in Tokyo's Setagaya ward. She is also known as the author of several books, including *My Lantern* and *Sliding Doors.* Matsuda remembers her lovingly.

"She really was a wonderful Christian, as well as a great educator. She always longed for the peace of the world. Even during the war, she firmly maintained her attitude as an ardent advocate of everlasting peace in the world. That was why she was closely watched by the authorities during the war, as a dangerous person, together with other famous Christian pioneers, such as Mr. Kanzo Uchimura, founder of the *Mukyokai,* an independent Christian movement in Japan, and his successor, Professor Tadao Yanaibara, of Tokyo University, later president of that prestigious school."

Michi Kawai was uncompromising in her witness of Jesus Christ. When she applied for government approval to start a college during the jingoistic days of World War II, officials of the Ministry of Education pressed her to omit any reference to the Christian faith. But Miss Kawai prayed silently the prayer of Martin Luther,

"Here I stand. God help me."

In a day when many a Christian leader bowed to government pressure, Michi Kawai stood her ground. Her application to open a college explicitly "founded on Christian principles" was approved.

But what Matsuda-san especially remembers about Michi Kawai is her concern for people.

"Miss Kawai was a very busy person, but she never failed to extend sympathy and consolation to those who suffered mentally or physically or were plunged into worry and grief. I still remember how thankful and happy I was when she came to see me in the hospital where I was laid up with pleurisy. The joy of seeing her and the gratitude I felt for her warm consolation were more than I could express.

"No matter how busy she was, when she heard of someone suffering, either mentally or physically, she could not help showing her sympathy in some way or other. Either she would pay a visit, or if she couldn't find time, she always wrote letters of consolation to the person who was suffering."

This was an important factor in Matsuda-san's conversion, as she herself testifies: "In this way I was made to understand what real Christian love is."

But Kiyoko-san's path into the company of believers was not strewn with cherry blossoms.

"My family was very strongly against my entry into the Christian church. Because of their opposition I just couldn't realize my hope for baptism."

Grandmother was a formidable obstacle. But she was not alone. Her entire family was opposed to the step Kiyoko-san was contemplating.

Who could help young Kiyoko-san find the internal strength to rise above the tradition of compliant obedience to her family? Who could give this slender young girl the fortitude to deny all Confucian ideals and defy her family?

Miss Michi Kawai was the human instrument God used. She was a woman of great talent. Like Umeko Tsuda and Caroline Macdonald she was a person of strong character. The writer remembers an evening at the home of Miss Michi Kawai soon after his arrival in Japan as a new missionary in the postwar period. Miss Kawai herself prepared and served the tasty *sukiyaki* dinner in her *tatami*-floored Japanese home. Elegant in a grey Japanese kimono, she was at home in her Japanese culture. She was also definite and articulate in her opinions. Her wit flashed in impeccable English.

The Bryn Mawr years and the Scottish determination of Caroline Macdonald had reinforced her native strength of mind and will. It was very clear to this young missionary that he was in the presence of a remarkable woman.

In one of her books Michi Kawai reveals a secret of her accomplishments when she exclaims, "Persistency, thou art a jewel!"

Some of her determination must have entered the soul of young Kiyoko-san.

"I attended a summer conference of the YWCA," Matsuda-san recalls, "while Miss Kawai was there as president of the association.

"At last, I could make up my mind to become a Christian and be baptized, though I foresaw strong opposition from our family."

How deep-seated was that opposition became dramatically clear. In a previous chapter Matsuda-san has described how even a bloodthirsty samurai waving a curved and crimsoned Japanese sword could not disturb the composure of this remarkable woman. Yet there was one exception.

"The only time I ever saw Grandmother lose her temper was when I told her that I should like to become a Christian.

"Without uttering a word, she just snatched the Bible from my hand and threw it into the kitchen fire."

Kiyoko-san stood pale and helpless watching the flames of the *irori*, the open kitchen fireplace, consume her beloved Bible. The iron teakettle that always hung suspended from the smoke-darkened rafters soon began to sing.

But fortified by the courage she drew from her faith in Jesus Christ and from strong Michi Kawai, Kiyoko-san at 18 took the decisive step and was baptized.

The longed-for event took place in the Presbyterian Fujimicho Church, largest and most influential in the empire.

The pastor poured the water of baptism on her dark head bowed over the baptismal font, as he intoned the words of Holy Baptism:

"Kiyoko Matsuda, I baptize you in the name of the Father and of the Son and of the Holy Spirit."

Who can guess what were the human anxieties and the exalted motions of the Spirit of God in Kiyoko-san's soul in that moment of victory? But this is holy ground, and here we take off the shoes from the curious feet of our inquiry.

The voice belonged to none other than the Rev. Masahisa Uemura, one of the great patriarchs of the Christian church in Japan.

Kiyoko-san was fortunate to find herself under the shepherding of Uemura-sensei. He was a Christian samurai in the full sense of the term. He was not only a good pastor but a unique and distinguished preacher. In the pulpit he employed special expressions of Japanese style that were not used by foreign missionaries. He "Japanized" what he had learned from Western Christianity and developed a native theology for his own country.

But like the samurai he was, Uemura-sensei was utterly

loyal to His Lord Jesus Christ and to Biblical Christianity. He used to say:

"Christianity without miracles would be Christianity without Christ. Christianity without Christ would no longer be Christianity."

The greatest theological controversy in the history of Japanese Christianity occurred in 1901 when Uemura opposed Danjo Ebina, a celebrated scholar and orator. To the credit of the Japanese church it must be affirmed that the only serious controversy it has ever spent time on dealt with the central issues of the Gospel. For Ebina's theology was unitarian. Christ was no more than human, and His death was not an atonement for sin. Uemura refused to give an inch.

"The deity of Christ and His redemption are the two essentials of preaching."

Hidenobu Kuwada, a recent president of Tokyo Union Theological Seminary, pays tribute to Pastor Uemura:

"We must be grateful to him for maintaining such an orthodox evangelical view in that time of modern liberal theology."

But Uemura was no narrow exclusivist. He led in many kinds of Christian cooperation. Earnestly, he sought to overcome the handicaps of Western denominationalism by trying to unite the Presbyterian and the Congregational churches.

When some tradition-minded Southern Presbyterian missionaries complained about Uemura's choice of a moderate textbook in systematic theology at Meiji Gakuin Theological Seminary in Tokyo, he resigned his professorship in 1903 and established an independent theological seminary near Fujimicho Church. He did not rely on subsidies from the West. The students paid tuition instead of receiving scholarships. Uemura helped poor students, but he never allowed parasites to take advantage of his generosity.

This seminary became the site of Tokyo Union Theological Seminary formed during World War II when many Protestant denominations united in one Church of Christ in Japan. After the war, the seminary moved to its present location next to the International Christian University in Mitaka, a Tokyo suburb. Among insiders, it is still known as "the Uemura seminary."

The Fujimicho building, which housed a Uemura memorial room, became the Tokyo Lutheran Center. It swarms like a beehive with numerous activities, including the headquarters of the Japan Lutheran Hour. Here Matsuda-san was employed for a time as translator at the old familiar site first established by the pastor who baptized her.

No doubt she thought back often to those Sundays after her baptism at 18, when she sat in the pew of Fujimicho Church and heard her pastor preach in this vein:

"What is sin? Is it worldly desires, troubles, punishments, absurdity, debt in the spirit, for which we should be responsible? No, it is beyond such things. Sin is the fact of our being separated from God." Such a view of sin was Biblical in conception and was like that of the great Reformers Martin Luther and John Calvin.

But Pastor Uemura never stopped there. As a great evangelist he hastened to preach Jesus Christ and Him crucified and risen again.

"We all have sinned and come short of His glory. We are justified freely by His grace through the redemption in Christ Jesus. God loved us so deeply that He gave His only begotten Son that whosoever believes in Him should not perish."

With utmost clarity, Uemura-sensei distinguished forgiveness from its fruits.

"We are not forgiven because we have been influenced and so become righteous by the death of Christ. We should distinguish between forgiveness and its results. Forgiveness goes back beyond every kind of virtue. It comes only from God, from His everlasting love to us."

As a wise theologian, Pastor Uemura understood that the division between Law and Gospel in the Scripture does not allow one to separate Bible passages neatly into two separate stacks. The same event may be both condemnation and salvation, as he explained:

"Thus the crucifixion was forgiveness. But it is, at the same time, the judgment given us in Christ. We should bear it in mind that the crucifixion has such a twofold meaning. In that event we were judged and saved by God. We died and were born again in Christ. We can never bear good fruits of righteousness until we are newly born in the Spirit. At the cost of Christ's life, we have been redeemed by God; hence we cannot help loving God and being faithful to Him."

Uemura-sensei was passionately devoted to Jesus Christ, uncompromising in what he believed to be right, and absolutely fearless in the proclamation of the Gospel.

Like many another person, Kiyoko-san at first may have thought him gruff, unsympathetic, even antagonistic, but as she got to know him better, she came to understand his devotion, his care, his kindness, and his love.

A great man was her pastor. He was the instrument God used to nurture and develop the faith to which she had committed herself.

Kiyoko-san pays tribute to another of the great cloud of witnesses who touched her life. This person played a special role at the font in Fujimicho church. Matsuda-san identifies her with love and admiration.

"When I was baptized, Miss Caroline Macdonald was my godmother. She also was a wonderful Christian."

Michi Kawai and Caroline Macdonald symbolize the many Christians from Japan and from across the sea whom God used to fuse and fashion Kiyoko Matsuda.

An unexpected tragedy in Tokyo changed the course of Caroline Macdonald's life. A young man named Yamada, not a Christian, but one who attended her Bible class, committed a terrible murder motivated by jealousy. Stunned by the news, she spent the night in prayer. The next morning found her knocking at the gates of the Tokyo jail, believing it was God's command for her to do so. It seemed to her that the young man's crime was her own. For she felt that it had been caused by the imperfection of her teaching. This reaction showed that she had learned from the Japanese their own intense feeling of *sekinin* — responsibility.

John McNab, Honorary Group Captain of the Royal Canadian Air Force, who has written her life story, recounts:

"To enter within the prison walls meant getting into the visiting line by six o'clock each morning. The prison authorities watched with amazement the coming and going of this frail Christian woman, who despite her other duties passed through the iron gates regularly to teach Yamada the Scriptures. Her faith and hope were contagious, the effect upon the murderer was a lesson to all."

Some time later the governor of the prison made a remarkable request:

"There are in the prison at this moment over thirty men who are awaiting the execution of the death sentence. I shall give you their names, and I want you to help them."

A great door had been opened to her. She visited those sentenced to die, sent them books, visited their families, and began a great social welfare work to society's outcasts. She helped released prisoners find jobs and opened a hostel where they could stay. Her deep plunge into human misery caused her to probe beneath the surface for the cause of such suffering. Her own answer was:

"The main cause of crime is selfishness. Selfishness not only of the individual but of society as a whole, the gulf fixed between rich and poor, the industrial system with its sweated labor and other scandalous conditions are largely to blame."

From Caroline Macdonald, Matsuda-san gained not only the Gospel of Christ but His heart of compassion as well. She relates:

"When Miss Macdonald saw that the Japanese YWCA could get along without her help, she just handed it over to Miss Kawai. And for the rest of her life she devoted herself to the rehabilitation of ex-convicts. I've heard it said that she was the only woman who was allowed to enter the cells of convicts all alone to talk with them."

The story of one of these remarkable converts is told in a book translated by Caroline Macdonald, *A Gentleman in Prison*. It contains the confessions of Tokichi Ishii, hardened criminal and murderer, written in Tokyo prison. When an innocent man was convicted for the murder of a *geisha* whom Ishii had killed, he found in himself enough decency to confess the crime. But he was not believed. Though tried, he was acquitted. Incredible as it may seem, he appealed the verdict and was eventually found guilty and sentenced to death. No doubt, he could take some justified satisfaction in his refusal to let another man die in his place. But in prison, Caroline Macdonald visited him and gave him a Bible. And there Ishii met his master. Idly, he began to read the story of Christ's passion. At once the difference between his own action and that of Christ became clear to him. Ishii knew himself to be a guilty murderer. But Jesus Christ was innocently crucified.

"Even I, hardened criminal that I was, thought it a shame that His enemies should have treated Him in this way."

Then, all unprepared, Ishii came upon the prayer of Jesus on the cross:

"Father, forgive them, for they know not what they do."
Ishii was transfixed.

"I stopped: I was stabbed to the heart, as if pierced by a five-inch nail. What did the verse reveal to me? Shall I call it the love of the heart of Christ? Shall I call it His compassion? I do not know what to call it. I know only that with an unspeakably grateful heart I believed. Through this simple sentence I was led into the whole of Christianity.

"I wish to speak now of the greatest favor of all—the power of Christ, which cannot be measured by any of our standards. I have been more than twenty years in prison since I was nineteen years of age, and during that time I have known what it meant to endure suffering, although I have had some pleasant times as well. I have passed through all sorts of experiences and have been urged often to repent of my sins. In spite of this, however, I did not repent, but on the contrary became more and more hardened. And then by the power of that one word of Christ, *Father, forgive them, for they know not what they do,* my unspeakably hardened heart was changed, and I repented of all my crimes. Such power is not in man."

For her amazing and unique service Caroline Macdonald received from the emperor of Japan the Sixth Order of the Sacred Treasure, and in 1924 the Department of Justice presented her with a gold cup bearing the Imperial Crest. A year later she became the first woman ever to receive the honorary degree of doctor of laws from her alma mater, the University of Toronto.

Strong Christians are made by God, but He uses other strong and remarkable Christians to help them. Kiyoko Matsuda is a product of the great age of the pioneers in the Christian church of Japan. There were giants in the earth in those days. With William Butler Yeats she could revel in her blessings and declare,

"I was very much blessed to have been allowed to meet so many fine Christian pioneers when I was young," she herself acknowledges today.

Though she is an invalid, what God has given her through others reminds her that she has a great Christian vocation not in spite of but because of her afflictions. She wants to pass on to other people the riches of strength and salvation that she received from the Spirit through a long procession of gifted saints who introduced her to the Christian faith and nurtured her in it.

"I feel that it is my responsibility to do my best, however humble it may be, for those suffering from disease or discouraged about their illness. I firmly believe that God wants me to help others until He calls me back to His home where there will be no pain or sorrow."

Amatsuchi mo

hito no kokoro mo

yawaragite

onozukara naru

haru no iro kana.

Melting heav'n and earth
And even the human heart,
Soft'ning ev'rything
By its own gentle power,
Comes the radiance of spring.

—Satoko Okawa

CHAPTER EIGHT

December Spring

Graduating from Tsuda College at twenty-one in 1912, Kiyoko-san returned to her quiet hometown in Ibaraki Prefecture. In geography the distance was only 50 miles, but in time it was more like 50 years. Yet she must have appreciated the slower pace and the preservation of old values in the country town with its neatly trimmed hedgerows and its straw thatched houses.

Yet soon she was off to the capital again. The neighbors were accustomed to hearing of Kiyoko-san's academic exploits. But this time they couldn't believe their ears. She was going to attend "Todai"—as Tokyo Daigakko is known by its students. This was Tokyo Imperial University, far and away the number one university of the nation. Todai had been founded to provide Japan with topflight leaders in all fields, especially in government. Nearly all the country's prime ministers have been graduates of Todai.

An unbelievable chance had come to Kiyoko-san. And with her mother's unfailing backing, she was quick to seize it.

Todai's president had taken a sensational step, extremely daring and radical for those times. He had opened the university's famed *akamon*—the "red gate"—to women students! The shocked gasps were heard all over a nation that had been dominated by males ever since the hard-riding Yamato horsemen had subjugated other clans 1,500 years earlier.

Having made such a bold advance, the president found it was necessary to compromise. The girls would be admitted only as special students. And they had to be college graduates. True, no entrance tests were given. But at the same time, the women were told that they would not be entitled to receive any graduate or undergraduate degrees from the university.

Matsuda-san was one of only ten women to be admitted to this stronghold of male chauvinism.

However, this feminine intermezzo turned out to be brief indeed. And Todai went back to its old status as an all-male school. Matsuda-san is not quite certain why the "akamon," the red gate, was closed to her sex once more. She theorizes,

"Perhaps it came about as a reaction from the side of the militarists and nationalists, who thought the whole idea of opening Todai to women was blasphemy. The general atmosphere in the country was in favor of women going back home to keep house and look after the family."

But there were others who wanted Kiyoko-san to have another opportunity. Her strength of purpose and her ability had not gone unnoticed at her alma mater.

One day a letter arrived from no less a person than Miss Umeko Tsuda, founder and president of her alma mater. She was asking Kiyoko-san's father to allow her to apply for a scholarship to Bryn Mawr, the same prestigious women's college on America's eastern seaboard that Umeko Tsuda and Michi Kawai had themselves attended.

If she could only go! Then her future, too, would read, "Ceiling unlimited!" It was too good to be true, an opportunity more fantastic even than her good fortune in being admitted to Tsuda College.

"But, alas! it was too late," writes Matsuda-san.

The heartbreak of that hour comes through in her words even today. It was matched only by another grief that had come to her a few months earlier.

"My mother, who had wished so much to have me study in America, suddenly died on February 22, 1914, at the age of only 42. Her death forced me to give up my long cherished desire to study at Bryn Mawr, though Miss Tsuda wrote and urged me to take the entrance examination even though it might appear impossible for me to go. That year was the only time a graduate of a college other than Tsuda got the Bryn Mawr scholarship. It had been intended for me.

"Had mother only been alive! It would have been the realization of a dream she had cherished from the time she had first shown me that newspaper picture of Japanese girls leaving for study abroad."

Kiyoko-san had to make the great renunciation of her life in order to be a dutiful daughter. The Confucian ethic expected it of her. And did not her newfound Christian faith into which she had been baptized only five years earlier have something to say about self-denial? A profound struggle went on within her. Could she bear to seek her life by losing it, as Jesus Himself had done? What kind of Christian witness would she give to her family if she left them in the lurch?

"I was the oldest of the children. My youngest brother was only two and a half. And though we had a good wet-nurse to take care of him, I had to stay home to help grandmother look after the family. That's why I had to give up my desire to study at Bryn Mawr."

In Japan children are nursed somewhat longer than in the West. In the old days, the lactation period lasted for three years or even more. Even today, in rural areas this lengthy extension of the breast-feeding period is not uncommon.

But for Kiyoko-san, her mother's death meant that she was denied a precious opportunity to drink at the fountain of knowledge in a fine school of the West. Quietly and without dramatics, drawing on the resources of her Christian faith and her samurai fortitude, Kiyoko-san remained at home.

Yet what seemed loss turned out to bring great gain from a most unlikely direction.

Grandmother Satoko Okawa preserved her lifelong samurai stoicism through all the wrenching loss of the person dearer to her than anyone else on earth.

"My mother was Grandmother Okawa's only child, the only prop of her old age. You can well imagine how great was her sorrow. But I never heard Grandmother weep or complain in front of other people after the funeral was over. She just bore the grief within herself."

But behind this facade a storm was convulsing her soul. Torn by inexpressible anguish, she felt herself drawn to the beckoning consolation of the despised Christian faith. Jesus Christ was drying the tears of granddaughter Kiyoko. Grandmother Okawa, drained by the intolerable effort required to present an emotionless mask to those around her, longed for the heart's ease that Kiyoko-san had found. But at the same time she felt a rising gorge of revulsion toward a foreign religion she had been taught to hate ever since she was a child. After all, Grandmother had been born under the old Tokugawa *sakoku* policy of isolation in force since 1639. For seven generations her ancestors had thought of Christianity as dangerous and un-Japanese.

During more than two centuries a Christian had all the social standing of a Communist in the United States — and considerably less personal security. The entire country was divided into cells of five families called *goningumi* by the government, with one man in each group responsible for reporting any Christian to the authorities. Whole villages at a time would be made to tread on the *fumie,* literally, a "stepping picture" of Christ on the Cross or of the Holy Child on His Mother's lap. The pictures were made in brass relief. Some of them may still be seen in the museums of Japan, the raised features of Jesus and Mary worn smooth as doorknobs by the thousands and millions of feet that trod upon them under the eyes of government officials in proof that they did not belong to Christ. So detested and hated and feared was the Christian faith! Those who refused to step upon the face of Jesus in denial of their Christian faith were executed, some by crucifixion and some by the sword. Others were suspended head down into pits of night soil, the human fertilizer that farmers used on their fields.

Much of that shame and disgrace still clung to Christianity in the new era.

The ice was rigid and unbending in Grandmother's heart. And yet, she began to have some doubts about the rightness of her hostility. Had not Granddaughter Kiyoko given up that outlandish plan of studying in America? Even though a Christian, had Kiyoko-san not proved her filial devotion and self-sacrifice for the family?

It was, in a sense, for the sake of her only daughter that Grandmother Okawa had endured the heartbreaking loss of her brilliant and promising young husband. And now that daughter was dead. With her, much of the meaning in Grandmother's life had died too. She needed a new center. But she did not know it.

Her grief was bitter as gall. Yet sweetness was around her. Kiyoko-san did not realize it, but her faith and life were influencing Grandmother Okawa.

The warm sun was shining on the stubborn ice choking the rivers of Grandmother's soul. The mild breezes were blowing.

To Kiyoko-san's utter amazement the miracle happened. The very loss of her only child which Grandmother Okawa had endured was employed by God to prepare this proud daughter of the samurai to surrender to Jesus Christ.

"I don't think she could ever have embraced the Christian faith but for this sad event," is Kiyoko-san's judgment today.

"The human instrument God used was the kind guidance of a Christian pastor who had persuaded Grandmother to send my sister to a mission school in Yokohama," Kiyoko-san goes on.

And so it came about that Grandmother Okawa, a true Japanese samurai woman of Tokugawa times, was baptized at 72! As Kiyoko-san watched, this cultured woman representing the best of the old tradition as well as its Spartan discipline, bowed her proud white head to receive the purifying water of baptism. Her granddaughter Kiyoko marvelled at the powerful grace of God which had wrought this miracle.

"My sister, who lived with Grandmother in her old age, told us that after she became a Christian she was meekness itself. Her stubbornness was entirely broken. She was always touchingly thankful for what she was given."

Grandmother lost nothing of what was best in her Japanese heritage. But now she had been gentled and purified.

Kiyoko-san admires her grandmother very much.

"She was talented in composing Japanese poems. Right after her baptism she expressed her joy of being saved by the grace of God in a lovely *waka*."

Within the strict discipline of 31 syllables, she said it all and made it sound as though she did not find the brief compass in the least confining:

Amatsuchi mo
hito no kokoro mo
yawaragite
onozukara naru
haru no iro kana

Melting heav'n and earth
And even the human heart,
Soft'ning ev'rything
By its own gentle power,
Comes the radiance of spring.

"How I wish I could convey the full meaning of her poem!" Matsuda-san yearns. "But my words are too short to express the full meaning of her poem. I'm an unworthy granddaughter."

Upon Kiyoko's graduation from Tsuda College, Grandmother Satoko Okawa had written a *waka* manifesting a literary quality equally high. But the attitude toward life and the world was very different:

Ikuhiro mo
kyo yori nobiyo,
hime komatsu!
Itoshinaki yo no
ne o katamete.

Like a sapling pine,
Keep on growing fathoms more,
Princess, than today.
In a world that pities not
Sink your roots, make them strong!

-Satoko Okawa

Interestingly enough, with all her expertise in Japanese poetry, Grandmother also came to appreciate Western hymnody. One of her favorites was a hymn written in 1824 by an American Episcopalian clergyman and hymn writer, William Augustus Muhlenberg (1796 – 1877), great-grandson of Henry Melchior Muhlenberg, "the patriarch of the Lutheran Church in America":

I would not live alway; I ask not to stay
Where storm after storm rises dark o'er the way.
The few lurid mornings that dawn on us here
Suffice for life's woes, are enough for its cheer.

I would not live alway; no, welcome the tomb;
Since Jesus hath lain there, I dread not its gloom.
There sweet be my rest till He bids me arise
To hail Him in triumph descending the skies.

But the hymn that Grandmother liked best was an original Japanese hymn set to a melody created in 1855 by George Frederick Root (1820 – 1895), an American composer best known for his Civil War songs. Matsuda-san provides a free translation of the poetic Japanese words found under Number 558 in the standard Japanese *Sambika*, literally "Songs of Praise," hymnal formerly used by most Protestant churches:

When the flowers are blown away,
The trees as fagots sold away,
When our house runs down
And we are forsaken by others,
On what can we depend?
To whom should we look for help?
To none but the loving friends
Created by God.

Three years after her baptism, Grandmother Okawa fell asleep in Jesus at the age of 75.

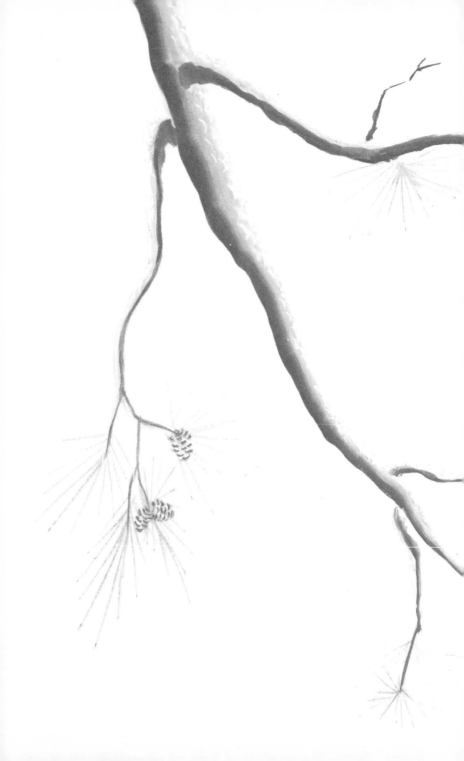

Me ni ureshi

   koigimi no sen

      mashiro nari.

What utter delight

   to the eye — my dearest one's fan,

      so perfectly white!

         —Taniguchi Buson (1715 — 1783)

CHAPTER NINE

Pleasure and Pain in Marriage

Though Kiyoko-san had to renounce the scholarship offered her at Bryn Mawr because of her mother's death, she did get the opportunity to go abroad after her marriage.

In Japan many marriages are still arranged by parents or other older persons. Sometimes this creates problems, but in many cases young people appreciate not being left entirely to their own resources. If a Christian girl marries a non-Christian husband, he may perhaps not allow her to attend church or to have their children baptized. Therefore Christian pastors sometimes endeavor to bring together Christian young people so that they may have the opportunity to found Christian homes.

A Christian pastor introduced Kiyoko-san to Hideo Matsuda. As time went on, they got to know each other well and were married. For the first time in three generations a woman of the Okawa family changed her name upon taking a husband. She now became Kiyoko Matsuda. Her bridegroom studied abroad, both in America and in Europe. In Belgium Kiyoko-san was a good helpmeet to him in the laboratory. In addition, her knowledge of French enabled her to interpret for her scientist husband in off-duty hours in the university town where they lived.

Through these experiences Kiyoko-san learned much that she could bring back to Japan. But she also brought much of Japan with her into the new situation. Her strict samurai upbringing on one occasion led to a very painful experience. She tells about their time together in Belgium in these words:

It was right after the end of the First World War when my husband was ordered to go abroad as a research student. He did part of his work at the University of California in Berkeley under the kind guidance of Professor Ernest Brown Babcock, a well-known scholar in genetics. The Babcocks were fine Christians. They looked after my husband with the tenderest care, especially when he underwent an operation on his appendix. We shall never be able to forget their self-forgetting devotion shown to us, especially to my husband.

But after about a year-and-a-half stay in Berkeley, California, my husband decided to go to Belgium to complete his research under Professor Victor Grégoire (1870–1938), a cytologist world famous for his knowledge of cell structures. He was a priest of the Roman Catholic Church but at the same time professor in the Agricultural Institute in Louvain. The city of Louvain is well known as the site of the famous university founded in 1426. Belgium is a small country, located between France and Germany, and Louvain is a quiet little college town well suited for study.

My husband was not entirely recovered from the after-effects of the operation. Besides, he couldn't understand French at all. Therefore, he wanted me to accompany him to Belgium, where only French and Flemish—a kind of Dutch dialect—were spoken. When we arrived, an American lady cytologist and another American cytologist and his family from Ithaca were already on hand, doing their research under the guidance of Professor Grégoire.

Belgium had not yet emerged completely from the devastation she had suffered during the First World War, and Louvain was one of the cities that suffered most terribly from the enemy attack. Most of the houses had been rebuilt with the indemnity paid by Germany, but here and there in the outskirts of the city we could still see ruins left unrepaired.

In the aftermath of the war, prices of commodities soared. The rate of exchange was most unfavorable. For one U. S. dollar we Japanese had to pay only two yen. But the Belgians had to give 33 of their francs, while the French were only a little better off at 25 francs to the dollar. One can imagine how the people were suffering from this vicious inflation, and I'm sure the financial conditions at the university were no exception.

But when we applied for admission to the laboratory as researchers, we were not asked to pay anything, not even for the materials we used in our research. They just welcomed us unconditionally into their laboratory, no discrimination being made between their own citizens and those of us who came from foreign countries.

We were well aware that Catholicism is the state religion of Belgium, and we were not surprised at all to find many priests and nuns wearing their black robes and habits, assiduously doing research work together with us lay men and women researchers. Professor Grégoire was a Catholic priest, but so unconventional as a priest we even detected something of the Bohemian in him. He reminded us of a Zen priest in Japan. But the janitor of the institute, with whom we were soon on intimate terms, told us that at home he was very severe in observing ascetic discipline. He would whip himself very hard at night for fear of inadequate practice of austerities. This seemed to me, a Protestant, very queer, but gradually as I came to accustom myself to the way of living

94

there, I began to notice a strong resemblance between the way certain Catholic priests discipline themselves and the way some of our Buddhist and Shinto devotees practice their austerities.

If you visit small shrines or temples in out-of-the-way country places in Japan, you'll often notice small hand-sewn toylike animals, mostly monkeys, hanging in front of a shrine. These show the worshiper's gratitude for wishes fulfilled. Sometimes they are given in hope of fulfillment. I noticed the same kind of offerings in Catholic churches in Belgium. Of course it is more than forty years since I visited that country, and things may have changed a great deal, but the offering of vows to God just as to Buddha is still going on, I'm sure.

Have you ever heard of *Okyakudo-maeri* in Japan? Literally, it means "one hundred times worship." If you will visit *Kannon-Sama*, the Buddhist Goddess of Mercy in Asakusa—a downtown shopping and amusement center of Tokyo—you will often notice women holding bundles of 100 paper strings walking around the temple (or shrine) one hundred times, offering prayers, and at each turn bending a string to make sure not to make mistakes in counting. This greatly resembles *neuvaine,* which the Catholic believers observe. While I was in Louvain, I one day paid a visit to the janitor, who had been laid up in bed with illness. He showed me the medal of *St. Therese de l'Enfant Jesus,* which he had put on the breast of his pajama, vowing to pray successively for nine days for his recovery through the intercession of this newly canonized beautiful young saint. Her family were such earnest and devout Catholics that all her sisters took the vows of nuns, and one of her sisters was the Mother Superior of a convent. St. Therese was the youngest, and she too took the veil. She had been very devout and faithful while she was alive. A miracle occurred, they say, when she died. That was why she was canonized. When I was in Louvain, she was the focus of public admiration and adoration. Don't you see the resemblance between the *Okyakudo-maeri* in our country and the Catholic *neuvaine?*

The loving devotion and adoration entertained by Roman Catholics for Mary, the mother of Jesus, is so deep that it is just unfathomable for us Protestants.

For instance, when Catholics are in deep grief, they kneel before the statue of Mary and confide everything to her, asking her to show them how to survive their afflictions. Or when they encounter difficult problems, they also kneel before Mary and pray her to help support them so that they may be able to face these challenges with courage. In all things, Mary plays such an important and indispensable role in their lives that for us it is really beyond our powers of comprehension. Mary is, so to speak, not only their guardian saint, but an adviser and confidant. The 18th of August is the Feast of the Assumption of St. Mary, the mother of Jesus, into heaven.

While I was in Louvain, I used to take lessons in French conversation from a woman whose husband, before his death, had been a professor at the University of Louvain. Once he was sent to Africa by the government on a special mission. While he was traveling in Congo, then a colony of Belgium, she had no anxiety about him because she firmly believed that Saint Mary would take good care of him. When I asked her why she didn't pray to God in Jesus' name, she replied,

"Jesus is God, so it is too awe-inspiring to ask God directly. Don't you think it's more natural to ask Mary, the beloved mother of Jesus, to intercede for us?"

I didn't ask her how and when her husband died, but after his death she attended the 6:00 a. m. mass without missing a single day. I asked her why she so assiduously observed the masses. You know, Belgium is situated in a high latitude. In wintertime it begins to get light as late as ten o'clock, and it becomes dark already at four in the afternoon. Her answer to my question was:

"I don't think my husband has been allowed to enter heaven yet. I believe he is still in purgatory. But if I continue to attend masses and pray for him here on earth, it will help him enter heaven sooner."

Here again I couldn't help noticing a strange similarity to the Buddhist thought prevalent in Japan. In our country whenever we visit the graveyard, our elders would take us before the *Jizo*, a guardian deity of children, and tell us to pick up pebbles and pile them up in front of the *Jizo*. They say when children die, they have to go to "Children's Limbo" where they are ordered to pile up pebbles, but when they at last pile them up, ogres come and throw the heaped-up pebbles down to the ground, and the children have to begin to pile them up all over again. But if we, on earth, pile pebbles in front of the *Jizo*, it helps alleviate the children's labors.

The *Bon* Festival is a kind of Buddhist All-Saints' Day observed from July 13 to 16. When *O-bon* comes around, we all go to our ancestors' graveyard to welcome their souls back home, and we never forget to visit *Jizo* and pile pebbles before him, to help the children in "the Children's Limbo." Don't you see the strong similarity between these two instances, the belief in purgatory and "the Children's Limbo" in Buddhism?

When I talk with Catholics, I'm always impressed by their unquestioning obedience to God and their firm belief in our general resurrection. Our practices and doctrines as Protestants may not entirely coincide with theirs, but we should respect their faith.

In former days when I was in Belgium two languages

were spoken, French and Flemish, a kind of Dutch dialect. In those days French was officially used, but in Louvain children had to learn two languages at school. In the hotel where we were staying, the garcons, or waiters, and mademoiselles spoke both languages freely, but there were few who could understand English. While in the laboratory my husband had no difficulty in conversing with the professor and the other researchers as they all understood and spoke English. But once outside the institute he could not make himself understood and had to depend entirely on my poor French.

Louvain is so close to Holland that, in some quarters, on one side of the street people spoke Flemish while on the opposite side they spoke French.

Louvain is so near the Netherlands that the people's way of life strongly resembles that of Hollanders. You know Dutch people are well known for making war on dirt, and the Belgians living in the regions adjacent to Holland are likewise very fond of cleanliness. On Saturdays, passing those quarters we would see women wearing *sabots,* or wooden shoes, scrubbing not only the inside and outside of their houses but also even the stone-block paved sidewalks in front of their houses.

The children look forward with mingled eagerness and dread to St. Nicholas Day on December 6. On the eve of this festival, mother and father prepare presents for their children, just as parents in Protestant countries do at Christmastime. The presents St. Nicholas brings are mostly cakes made of chocolate. At the beginning of December all the confectioners' shops display all sorts of chocolate cakes to be given to children on St. Nicholas Day. They say St. Nicholas was a kind saint who loved children very much and brings nice presents to good children, but to naughty ones he brings a whipping.

I know very little about the administration of hospitals

abroad. In Japan nearly all hospitals have resident doctors who stay in the hospital at all times. Nurses remain in the hospital, night and day, in three shifts of eight hours even at midnight. I don't want to generalize about hospitals in Belgium, but at least in the sanatorium in which I was a patient, there were no resident doctors. The nurses were all nuns, who would leave the sanatorium in the evening for the vesper worship service. The doctors came from outside the hospital, from the department of medicine of the university, to examine and treat the patients. On Sundays neither doctors nor nurses were around. This was a day of devotion and prayer for the nuns. Only young assistant-nurses remained in the sanatorium to take care of the patients. It was fortunate that I wasn't seriously ill. Still, I could not help feeling lonely and uneasy.

After consultation, a young doctor from the medical department of the university told me that in order to confirm his diagnosis, it might be necessary to apply an instrument. I had already experienced the use of that instrument when I was in Japan. As it had given me little pain, I had no anxiety about the use of the instrument. But the young doctor did not have a gentle touch. He had little experience in the handling of the instrument. It gave me terrible pain. But all the while my grandmother's words kept ringing in my ears:

"Behave calmly and quietly as becomes a Japanese woman. Don't you behave shamefully when you are outside of Japan!"

I just bore the pain without uttering a word. But there is a limit to human endurance. All of a sudden I fainted. I was told later that the doctor and the nurse were very much upset.

Afterwards, my husband scolded me. "If you don't know how to express the word 'painful' in French, why don't you cry out either in English or even in Japanese and say 'Itai'?

There is a limit to behaving properly. Don't you know the proverb, 'When in Rome, do as the Romans do'?"

Yes, I know how to say "painful" in French, but I just couldn't say it. That time my grandmother's discipline left me in a sad plight.

Upon his return to Japan Kiyoko-san's husband earned the degree of doctor of agriculture at Tokyo Imperial University. He taught at various colleges and died at 81 years of age.

Dr. Matsuda came from an illustrious family in Nagasaki. His grandfather also was a scientist and patented the canning process in Japan. Equally progressive in business, he fathered the canning industry in Japan in 1871 with a factory for canning fish in Nagasaki. Mrs. Matsuda wrote in one of her letters:

"I've long wished to introduce him and his work to your country but least dreamed of writing about myself. My husband's grandfather also established the first English school in Nagasaki. It drew ambitious young men from all over Japan."

Dr. Matsuda himself was very artistic with ink and brush. He favored his family and friends with gifts of his *sumie*, or charcoal ink paintings in the form of Japanese scenes. It is an art he learned from his father before him.

Mrs. Matsuda is taller than her husband was. The Japanese call this colloquially a *nomi no fufu*, or "flea couple." The Matsudas laughingly confided this popular expression to Paul and Carol Kreyling, missionaries of The Lutheran Church—Missouri Synod, who find themselves in the same situation relative to height. Mrs. Matsuda also interpreted for Paul at one time.

Kazuo, eldest of their three sons, followed in his father's footsteps and graduated from Tokyo University. Like his father, he earned the title of doctor of agriculture. He teaches at Tohoku State University in Sendai. At the invitation of the chemistry department he carried on study and research at the University of Ohio.

It is a glory in any Japanese family if even one son passes the severe entrance examination and graduates from Tokyo University. This distinction came twice to the Matsuda family. Second son Norio is also a graduate of that famous school. Like his elder brother he also earned a doctor's degree. His specialty is pharmacology. Today he serves as a consultant on medicine to various companies in Japan.

Third son Teruo is chief engineer in charge of sulphate pulp at the Juyo Paper Manufacturing Company.

The eldest daughter is a music teacher in a primary school.

The Matsudas have eight grandchildren and five great-grandchildren.

The eldest grandson, a graduate of Keio University, one of the finest private universities in Japan, is likewise doing well. His grandmother wrote: "He is now in Moscow, negotiating with the Russian Government on a pipeline to import oil from Russia."

The Matsudas have also reared grandson Shigeo. Though accepted also at Tokyo University, he elected to attend the International Christian University. Grandmother Matsuda was pleased at his choice. She is overjoyed that he has confessed his faith in Jesus Christ, has been baptized, and takes an active part in Musashino Lutheran Church in Suginami Ward of Tokyo, which she also attends.

Education and faith in Jesus Christ have been the twin concerns of Kiyoko Matsuda's life. And both motifs may be traced in her descendants, who rise up and call her blessed.

Since by my carelessness or ignorance

I do my body needless harm and wrong,

Here I shall magnify this second chance

to recreate it, healthy, pure, and strong.

—*Songs of the Sanitarium*
William Merrell Vories Hitotsuyanagi

CHAPTER TEN

"White Flowers"

Clinical Card of Mrs. Kiyoko Matsuda

First applied for consultation Aug. 22, 1957, to the Second Department of Oral Surgery, School of Dentistry, Tokyo Medical and Dental College.

Chief complaint: Swelling in the lower jaw.

Diagnosis: Gingival swelling of the mandible.

Operation I. Aug. 25, 1957. Extraction of teeth and curettage of the swelling under local anesthesia by Dr. Miyagawa.

Operation II. March 1960. Felt the recurrence of the aforementioned symptoms, entered Kanto Rosai Hospital, and underwent an operation of the affected lower jaw. (Details unknown, probably removal of the necrotic bone.)

Operation III. July 1, 1960. Again entered the Second Department of Oral Surgery, School of Dentistry, Tokyo Medical and Dental College.

Diagnosis: 37. 7. 4. No. 15680. Spindle cell sarcoma. After the operation, treatment with cobalt 60. 5,000 roentgen irradiation.

1961. Mental gingival swelling. As pre-operative measure, X-ray treatment of 1,000 roentgen for 8 days.

Operation IV. June 21, 1961. Assistant Professor Tokiwa carried out a partial removal of the mandible.

Diagnosis: 36. 7. 4. No. 17417. Necrotic spindle sarcoma.

Operation IVA. Sept. 13, 1961. Removal of the necrotic bone by Asst. Prof. Tokiwa. Implantation of metal plate.

Operation V. October 1963. Again the removal of mandibular bone by Asst. Prof. Tokiwa. The left ramus remains unremoved.

Operation VI. December 1963. Sudden bleeding. X-ray investigation showed it was caused by a tumor in the abdomen. Underwent a laparotomy. Artificial anus made. (Jan. 10, 1964)

Operation VII. Surgery for intestinal obstruction. (March 1964)

Operation VIII. 1965. Entered Toranomon Hospital. Hemimandibulectomy — the remaining half of the right jaw entirely removed by Professor Ueno of the First Department of Oral Surgery, School of Dentistry, Tokyo Medical and Dental College.

Operation IX. 1967. Swelling under the left jaw. Entered the First Department of Dental Surgery. Excision of tumor. Removal of the remaining left ramus by Professor Ueno.

Operation X. Swelling under left ear removed. After the operation, referred to the radiology department to treat swelling of the left auricular region. Radiation therapy, using betatron electron beam.

April 1 — May 13, 5,000 rads. to the left pre-auricular swelling. Afterwards, redness and dry disquamation caused by irradiation therapy. The swelling has disappeared.

February 1972
Gradual swelling of infra-auricular region.
Second treatment of electron beam therapy by betatron.
Treatment February 18 and still continuing.

Matsuda-san's trouble began in low key.

She paid little attention to it at the time. Ruefully she confesses: "By my own carelessness and ignorance I did my body needless harm and wrong, as William Merrell Vories has said. His words fit my case only too perfectly. I did not realize in the least what a serious mistake I had made in failing to take the disease seriously at the outset."

She urges this most emphatic word of advice on her fellow-sufferers:

"Don't underestimate your disease!"

When Matsuda-san first noticed a swelling in her lower jaw, it gave no pain at all. She thought little about it. But finally she went to the Department of Oral Surgery at the School of Dentistry of the Tokyo Medical and Dental College. Doctor Miyagawa examined her and declared,

"It's nothing serious. You can have it taken care of as an out-patient."

He proceeded to scrape the swollen gums of the lower jawbone.

But since Matsuda-san was already past sixty, she asked Dr. Miyagawa to let her stay in the hospital until she was well again. After a week she was allowed to go home.

For a time all went well.

"But after a lapse of three years I felt the return of the same symptoms. But the surgeon's words 'nothing serious' were indelibly engraved upon my mind. And then and there I made a great and irrevocable mistake.

"A dentist friend of my second son heard about my case. He offered to do the operation, since it was nothing serious. Had I only known what oral surgery really involves, I would never have accepted his offer. I did not realize then what arduous training and long experience are necessary for a doctor to become a full-fledged oral surgeon.

"But as it was, I accepted his offer and had the operation done by my son's friend.

"Alas! The symptoms recurred after only three months. Of course, it was entirely my own fault for failing to realize that he was not an oral surgeon but simply a dentist unqualified to undertake such an operation.

"This was the beginning of the long, tormenting history of my disease that was to cost me dearly."

Now thoroughly frightened, Matsuda-san returned at once to Dr. Miyagawa, who had performed the first operation. Without delay, she underwent surgery for the third time.

After the operation, Dr. Miyagawa approached her with a grave expression. She heard the dread words:

"I'm sorry to have to tell you that there was some malignancy.

"Because only three months have elapsed since the

second operation, the adhesions were so great that I just can't guarantee the complete eradication of the malign agent.

"I recommend cobalt 60 treatments as a precautionary measure."

Matsuda-san received an irradiation of 5,000 roentgens of cobalt 60.

Nine months passed, months of uncertainty and anxiety.

But then the old telltale swelling recurred just as the surgeon had feared.

Once more Matsuda-san had to overcome her dread and bring herself to go back to the Tokyo Medical and Dental College hospital. Dr. Miyagawa, who performed the previous surgery, had left the hospital staff.

Now surgery began to get more serious. Assistant Prof. Tokiwa performed operation number 4 on June 21, 1961. He cut away nearly one-third of the lower jawbone. Then he engrafted the very bone he had cut away after first exposing it to 5,000 roentgens. It was his hope that the bone graft would be successful.

But less than three months later, on September 13, Mrs. Matsuda found herself on the operating table again. The ingrafted section of bone had died. It had to come out. Instead Dr. Tokiwa now inserted a special thin metal plate.

"If we don't encounter any trouble," he explained, "that plate can remain in your mouth indefinitely in place of the bone that we had to remove. It's made of a special kind of metal that will do no harm even in your mouth."

But this too proved to be a disappointment in the long run and finally had to be removed.

Otherwise, the next two years passed uneventfully. But with dramatic suddenness, the disease that was silently at war against her body attacked on another front. In mid-December 1963 Matsuda-san encountered the severest test her body and her spirit had yet known.

"In the middle of the night I woke up with sudden bleeding. In the morning I was taken to the hospital. Various X rays revealed the cause of the bleeding—a tumor in my abdomen. If left untreated it might develop into cancer.

"As a result I underwent a laparotomy. An artificial anus was made."

But another even more serious problem was lying in ambush. An obstruction developed in the bowel.

Once again it was a sudden emergency. Matsuda-san had to undergo another operation at once.

But as only three months had passed since the last operation, the doctors had to perform surgery under local anesthesia.

"I did not lose consciousness. I was aware of all that was going on. When the entire intestine was taken out, oh! the pain was past endurance. At last the operation was over. I felt a cold chill when the blood transfusion began. I remember calling out asking them to cover me up. And then I fell into a coma."

Matsuda-san almost slipped away into eternity at this point.

"While lying unconscious I found myself on an open meadow, all green, dotted here and there with beautiful white flowers. I was running about barefoot, carefree, and gleeful as a child. And I was asking myself over and over,

" 'How is it that I can run about so freely? What has become of my limping foot?'

"You see, I had broken my hip in 1952, and ever since I have had to walk with a cane."

Afterwards, Matsuda-san was told that her postoperative condition had been all but hopeless. Even the doctors had all given her up. All her relatives were summoned to the hospital to make their farewells at what they believed to be her deathbed.

"While I lay in this condition at the brink of the grave, my youngest son heard me mumble faintly, *'shiroi hana'* — 'white flowers.'

"I could neither eat nor drink anything at all, not even a drop of water. Due to extreme malnutrition, I was so terribly weak and exhausted that I had to depend entirely on intravenous feeding.

"They had to give me six or seven bottles. Nearly all available veins from my arms to my feet were used up for the insertion of the needles. The doctors were hard put to find any suitable veins.

"Worst of all, the incisions that had been sewn up refused to heal. They parted asunder. They failed to heal until I could regain some measure of physical stamina. Therefore I had to stay in the hospital nearly ten months."

As time went on, Matsuda-san learned from those around her further details of her narrow brush with death.

"In the hospital where I underwent surgery, it was customary to keep the most serious cases after the operation in a room right next to the nurses' station so that the nurses could keep vigil over them. I was wheeled to that room. Two other patients were already there, but of the three I was regarded as being in the most critical condition, as I was still in a coma.

"One of the patients was an elderly lady who didn't seem so very badly off. In the morning she even had her breakfast, but in the afternoon she suddenly passed away, while I still lay in a coma. Her husband, who was looking after her, bade farewell to my son, who was sitting at my bedside.

" 'I thought it was your mother who would go first.'

"My son was at a loss what to answer.

"The other old man in the same room died too. I was the only one of the three who lived.

"When I was told of this upon regaining consciousness, I felt keenly that there must be something that God wills me to do. I made up my mind to try my best to get well.

"When I got much better, I tried to move my head, but I found, to my dismay, that I could not. In Japan when someone is very seriously ill, we say, 'Mr. So-and-So is so very sick that he cannot lift his head.' Now I came to understand for the first time how true this saying is. When the nurse helped me lift my head, I could raise the rest of my body. But when I tried to lift my head all by myself, I found it absolutely impossible to do so."

But feeble as she was, Matsuda-san put her samurai determination to work in the effort to get better.

"I asked the nurse to fix a strong cord at the end of my bed. By holding the other end of the cord I tried to raise myself. I attempted it many times but always failed. I was too weak. But by sheer perseverance, I succeeded in the end."

With the enemy at bay in this sector, Matsuda-san was forced to take up the battle once more against her archfoe, cancer of the jawbone. She had to subject herself to two more operations, sacrificing nearly the entire left side of her lower jawbone. Thus far, the right side was in no way affected.

But one day Matsuda-san ran her tongue along the right side of her lower jawbone and to her horror discovered the same frightening symptoms of sarcoma.

The shock was great, but so was her courage.

"I made up my mind to do whatever I could to protect myself against this disease. I determined to find the topmost oral surgeon in all of Japan and ask him to undertake what I hoped would be the final operation. I wanted someone I could fully depend on.

"Eventually, I discovered that the one man who could help me in my sad plight was Professor Ueno of Tokyo Medical and Dental College Hospital.

"I asked him to come over to the hospital where I was being cared for. Fortunately, he consented to come."

This operation, she knew, would be drastic. There could be no halfway measures this time. Matsuda-san was uneasy.

Among her relatives, there are some ardent Roman Catholic Christians. While she was in the hospital, they visited her and tried to persuade her to convert to Catholicism. But Matsuda-san stood firm in her Protestant faith of half a century. Yet she deeply appreciates the concern of her Roman Catholic sisters in Christ. She pays tribute to them, saying:

"We should draw a lesson from their meek attitude of implicit obedience to God."

Matsuda-san phoned some friends from the Women's Society of the Musashino Lutheran Church to which she now belongs. This she did, not because of any apprehension about the impending surgery, but rather from reflection upon herself. Would she be able to stand before God if she were called away by Him at that moment?

Her sisters in the faith gathered around her hospital bed. They prayed with her. They comforted her. And then they sang in Japanese,

"Just as I am without one plea,
But that Thy blood was shed for me,
And that Thou bidd'st me come to Thee,
O Lamb of God, I come, I come."

Encouraged by the hymn, Matsuda-san set out once more on the all-too-familiar way to the operating room. She was taken to Toranomon Hospital in Tokyo, near the American embassy.

This operation, her eighth, was Draconic indeed. The remaining half of her right jaw was entirely removed. A nose, ear, and throat specialist assisted Professor Ueno. At one point he performed a tracheotomy, cutting open Matsuda-san's throat to help ease her breathing by inserting an instrument in the windpipe.

The specialist was of the opinion that Matsuda-san would never be able to speak intelligibly again.

However, he had not reckoned with her Christian faith and her samurai spirit.

"As soon as I was well enough to sit up in bed, I began to practice pronouncing Japanese words. And I tried to read books and newspapers aloud. In this way I gradually regained the power of speech and could make myself understood fairly well."

Her doctors regarded her accomplishment as a medical phenomenon.

That linguistic achievement was no empty triumph of willpower. By it God magnified Matsuda-san's witness to her fellow sufferers at Toranomon Hospital as well as to many others upon her release.

Two years later, a swelling appeared under her left jaw. It proved to be a tumor, which had to be cut away. Together with it, Professor Ueno removed her remaining left jawbone.

Just before this operation, Matsuda-san's doctors decided to preserve for medical history a record manifesting the speaking ability of such jawless patients. Bringing in a tape recorder, they asked Matsuda-san to read short passages in her impressive linguistic repertoire of Japanese, English, French, German, and Russian.

On this most unusual tape recording Matsuda-san recited one of her favorite English poems, "Crossing the Bar," the very last verses written by Alfred Lord Tennyson before his death. The poem expressed the deep feelings of Mrs. Matsuda's own heart.

> Sunset and evening star,
> And one clear call for me!

And may there be no moaning of the bar,
When I put out to sea,

For tho' from out our bourne of Time and Place
The flood may bear me far,
I hope to see my Pilot face to face
When I have crossed the bar!

Modestly, Matsuda-san reports, "It might not have been very well pronounced, but at least I thought I could read fairly well. As to German and Russian I really cannot boast, as I began to study them in my late seventies."

Again the doctors thought that the operation would put an end to her speaking. But once more, and in the face of mounting odds, Matsuda-san's indomitable spirit proved the predictions of the best medical experts too pessimistic.

The ninth operation made a difference in Matsuda-san's speech that would be obvious to anyone listening to the multilingual tape recording made just on the eve of that surgery. But she is still able to communicate intelligibly — and even in foreign languages.

In January 1970 Matsuda-san came to visit the writer and his family at the Tokyo Lutheran Center. We spent an unforgettable afternoon conversing with her, mostly in English. We were surprised how well she could communicate.

Through all the many battles in her long campaign against cancer Matsuda-san carried a secret weapon.

"What sustained me was the conviction that God is faithful and that He would not allow me to be tempted beyond my strength but would with the temptation give me strength to endure it and so provide me with a way out.

"In spite of all the inconveniences caused by the loss of various organs, I'm happy and full of thankfulness that my inner eyes have been opened more clearly than ever.

"While I was healthy I never dreamed what a wonderful blessing it is to be able to eat, swallow, and speak. But once deprived of the normal use of these functions, I now truly admire God's wonderful creation.

"For example, once deprived of the lower jaw, even the tongue will not act properly. You can't imagine with what difficulty I swallow my daily food, even though it is all liquid or semiliquid. I can't swallow a pill. No matter how small it is, the tongue won't send it down the throat."

Matsuda-san's husband was something of a gourmet cook. Paul and Carol Kreyling, longtime missionaries of The Lutheran Church—Missouri Synod, recall the delicious Nagasaki Chicken he prepared for them in Chinese style when they were guests at the Matsuda home.

Matsuda-san's eldest son was taking supper with her one evening. He could not help observing, "Mother, I'm glad that this unhappy lot has come to you and not to Father. He would never be able to stand the kind of life you lead."

Matsuda-san admits that it is no picnic.

"Most older people, though they are neither gluttons nor gourmets, find pleasure in eating good food and delicacies.

"Yes, it really is dull and insipid to have to take one's daily meals in liquid form. But I deem it a genuine blessing that I can at least gain enough nourishment to sustain my body.

"It will be hard for you to understand how inconvenient it is not to be able to make oneself understood by speaking. For instance, now I can't take a taxi by myself. However hard I try, I can never explain to the driver clearly enough where I want to go.

"When I go out shopping, I must write down what I want and how much I want, and then show the slip to the shopkeeper."

Matsuda-san is a great lady. But she is also ready to talk about the realities.

"As to the artificial anus, I must always be on guard. For it lacks the contractile muscle needed for control.

"Now I have come to the conclusion that nothing can take the place of the organs we are born with. They are made with such extraordinary, exquisite delicacy that no human ability can replace them."

Why was Matsuda-san not spared these indescribable difficulties? Did she lack faith? Anyone who meets her soon knows that she is a woman whose faith runs deep and strong. Did she not pray God for healing?

"Whenever I prayed to be relieved of these trials, His answer was always, 'My grace is sufficient for you, for My power is made perfect in weakness.' "

She counts her blessings.

"Things I had previously taken for granted are now a source of deep gratitude to me. I still have eyes to see, ears to hear, and, though limping, I can walk about, doing my everyday household chores. What more can I wish for? I have nothing to grumble about."

Like some of her samurai ancestors, Matsuda-san has become a battlescarred veteran. After five operations performed under general anesthesia, and six more under local anesthetic, she is qualified to speak a word of courage to the green troops. Her behavior under such pitiless and unrelenting fire has gained the admiration of her doctors. Professor Ueno, the one who performed her last three operations, counseled her one day:

"We doctors can only *help* the patient get well. It is the will of the patient to get well that brings about the desired recovery.

"Since you have had to face death so many times and come out of it miraculously, I urge you to write down your experiences. They will surely prove very encouraging to those sick people who are living without hope."

For Matsuda-san faith in God does not mean passive resignation. It does not mean running up the white flag of surrender at the first onslaught.

"True, our life and our death are ordained by God. But so long as we are alive, we should do our best to preserve our life, the most precious gift of God."

Ripeness is all; her in her cooling planet

Revere; do not presume to think her wasted.

—William Empson, *To an Old Lady*

CHAPTER ELEVEN

"Ripeness Is All"

The *kaki* is a favorite autumn fruit in Japan. Persimmons in the Middle West are the size of table tennis balls or golf balls. But those of Japan are as big as tomatoes. If eaten even a few days too soon, the persimmon taste is astringent. One's mouth puckers up and feels most unpleasant. But if one waits until the proper time, preferably after the first frosts of the season, the persimmon is smooth and meltingly sweet, with no unpleasant aftertaste.

There is one variety that is not sweet even when it is picked in autumn. On the weathered walls of farmhouses one can see these *kaki* peeled and hung to dry well into the winter. But finally they become sweet and chewy as candy.

People who grow old are fortunate, not because of the length of their days, but because they have more opportunity to mature and ripen in Christian faith and character.

While the West idolizes youth and tries desperately to preserve it, the Orient has long venerated age and knows how to appreciate it. Not the green, not the most beautiful persimmon, but the ripe fruit is sweet.

Persimmons need a touch of frost to bring out their flavor. And Christians can often profit from a touch of suffering.

Matsuda-san is a sweet, frostbitten persimmon. She is

still bringing forth fruit in old age. And such rare fruit it is.

Pastor Masami Ishii, now teaching at Japan Lutheran Seminary in Mitaka, bears witness.

"Many who went to visit her in the hospital before her operations were struck by her composure. She was not centering anxiously on herself. She tried not to be a burden to the nurses and was worrying only about the other patients in her room. Wherever she is, she creates an atmosphere around her that breathes her love and faith."

Remembering the example of Michi Kawai, Matsuda-san went to visit other sick people so long as she was in any way able to do so.

In one of her letters, Matsuda-san wrote, "Last Saturday I went to visit a neighbor who is suffering from lung cancer. He seems so worried about his approaching surgery. But he appears to have taken courage after my short visit, as I told him that I had already undergone ten operations. So many around us are waiting for our help and consolation. May God give me health to serve these people!"

Her experience opened to Matsuda-san unique opportunities for Christian witness to persons in every walk of life.

Matsuda-san is witnessing Christ to a woman who had to endure the same drastic surgery she underwent.

"My present problem is how to console and lead into Christianity Mrs. M., a middle-aged lady who was my roommate while I was in the hospital. She suffered from the same disease I did, but, as you know, this disease gives no pain, and she was rather late in noticing it. Her lower jaw had to be taken away. As she hadn't expected such a drastic operation, she is in great despair. She seems nearly to have lost any wish to live.

"The other day I went to see her, and she just grasped my hands and would not let them go while the tears stood in her eyes.

"She is the wife of an editor of the *Mainichi Shimbun*, one of the most important daily newspapers in all Japan.

"I'm going to the hospital again on Monday. Then I'll bring her a book to give her consolation and hope. She is a Buddhist believer, but by the will of God I am sure she will some day be saved."

One can imagine what a shocking tragedy this kind of surgery would be for a woman in her middle years married to a successful and influential husband. This devastating loss of her beauty would be the sternest test of his love for her. Even if she recovers her strength, can she bring herself to go out in society?

Persistent and determined in mission work as in everything else during her long life, Matsuda-san is following up on her contract with despairing Mrs. M. She wrote:

"Yesterday I went to the hospital for a regular checkup and wanted to call on Mrs. M. But I was told that she had left the hospital. So when I got home, I phoned her and tried to speak to her, but I couldn't. She again was bedridden, so I told her mother to tell her not to lose heart, but to try to get well, since she is still young.

"The trouble is that we live far from one another, she in Omori nearer to Yokohama and I in Suginami. I'm not so well as before, and my boys won't let me go out alone. Wherever I go, someone must accompany me. It's only natural that they should be anxious about me. I'm now nearly 81.

"What I am thinking of now is to write her as often as possible and send her books that will give her comfort and encouragement and at the same time convey God's love to her.

"I already asked Pastor Aoyama, president of the Christian Publishing Company, to select some books desirable for those who haven't heard of the Gospel at all."

Three months later Matsuda-san's own condition had

worsened, but she continued to think of others rather than of herself. In mission as in courtship love will find a way. She reported on her progress:

"Since I'm not well enough to go out to visit and as Mrs. M. isn't well enough to see anyone, I wrote her several times and sent her a book, *There's the Way,* a kind of autobiography written by a Christian woman. The author was bedridden for seven years with tuberculosis of the spine. The book is one of the best sellers of late years, and I do hope Mrs. M. will find consolation, if possible, by God's help in Christ. I hope you'll join me in prayers for her."

Matsuda-san will surely see to it that Mrs. M. receives a copy of her own biography. As a matter of fact, she was moved to allow her story to be published not for her own glorification but to help other poor sufferers like Mrs. M.

"How happy I shall be if, under God's blessing, the book could be published at the earliest possible time in order to serve all the sooner those who suffer.

"Mrs. M.'s editor husband is a graduate in English literature. So when my book is published, I'm looking forward to sending it to him first of all.

"My only hope is that my manuscript may in some way be useful for those who suffer from illness."

One Christmas we received an especially meaningful letter from Matsuda-san. She had undergone a ninth operation with further impairment of her speech and other oral functions. But her letter was singing with Christmas joy:

"Have I told you the previous experience I've had with my niece Yuriko and her mother-in-law? I was taught through this that God will use even such a mean earthen vessel as I am to show His love to us.

"Yuriko had been seized with a coronary heart attack and had barely recovered from it. But she was in constant fear of death. One day I went to see her mother-in-law, who was an earnest believer in Buddhism. She said to me, 'I don't care for Christianity myself, so don't talk to *me* about it. But I'm worried to see Yuriko in continual fear of death. She always asks, "How can Aunt Matsuda be so happy and cheerful when she is suffering from such great physical handicaps?" So, if Yuriko, by embracing Christianity, could be as happy and cheerful as you are, I have no objection to her becoming a Christian. Please initiate her into Christianity.' "

Matsuda-san continues: "I was completely taken aback to hear such words coming from her. My heart was too full to say anything then and there. I wrote at once to the Japan Lutheran Hour to send Yuriko the Bible Correspondence Course. Her mother-in-law died as a Buddhist, but Yuriko was baptized and is now a member of our church."

Christians of the West may reflect on such a mature and fruitful Christian as Matsuda-san. She is an outstanding example of the new age of mutual sharing of the Spirit's gifts in the one body of Christ worldwide. As the Christians of Asia, Africa, and Latin America multiply and mature, they are encouraging and strengthening their brothers and sisters in the West. They are coming by jet plane or, as in Matsuda-san's case, via the printed page, as missionaries to Christians and non-Christians alike in the North Atlantic community. A new age of mission from six continents to six continents is coming into flower.

Carol Kreyling, whose husband, Paul, was a colleague of the writer in Japan, gives a remarkable instance of the way in which Matsuda-san influenced even Americans whose lives touched her own.

Betty, who loved to dance, was Matsuda-san's roommate at Toranomon Hospital. This young American DAC, a Department of the Army civilian employed by the U. S. forces, was in despair, as Carol reports.

"She had broken her hip while dancing at the nearby Sanno Hotel. Since the operation had not been too successful, the bones were not mending well. Amid great pain, Betty learned that one leg would now forever be shorter than the other."

"You will be able to walk again," the doctors told her, "with the help of a cane. But you will never dance again."

Carol Kreyling draws the similarities and the contrasts between the two hospital roommates.

"This happened just at the same time when Dr. Ueno told Mrs. Matsuda that she would never speak again. The American woman was depressed, for dancing had been her whole life. She lamented and complained to her Japanese partner.

"Mrs. Matsuda wrote notes to Betty in English in an attempt to bring her out of her depression. She shared her Christian faith with the young woman."

Later, Betty confessed to the Kreylings, "I would never have had the will or the desire to get well if it had not been for the courage that Mrs. Matsuda instilled in me.

"As I lay in bed and heard Mrs. Matsuda doggedly practice her speaking, breaking through with an English word from time to time, I made up my mind to walk again too."

Betty was released to her small rented house. Mrs. Matsuda gave the Kreylings her address. They invited her to attend the English language Christmas church service held at that time in the Star Lounge of the Tokyo Hilton Hotel.

"Because of the Christian faith that Mrs. Matsuda had shared with her, Betty went to church for the first time in over three years. She had tears in her eyes as she once again worshiped her Savior Jesus Christ.

"God works in mysterious ways to bring His message to the hearts of men," Carol reflects. "A woman who is told she would never walk straight again and a woman who is told she would never speak again meet in the miracle of God's healing. Perhaps the healing was not the complete physical restoration of the body. But the healing of the self is the true miracle."

Matsuda-san uses her thorn in the flesh not as an occasion for self-pity but as a missionary tool in reaching out to comfort and evangelize other sufferers. She belongs to the company of those who are more than conquerors through Him who loves us. Such maturity in faith and love is more than healing.

Kiyoko Matsuda understood very well that Christian love and witness are not for export only. She did not reserve them for her contacts outside the home, say at church or in public. Her Christian love began right at home though it did not end there.

Carol Kreyling relates her impression of the aging Matsudas.

"In their later years the Matsudas were—how shall I say it? Some might have called them pathetic. And yet, because they did not exhibit self-pity one did not look upon it as pathetic. Let's say 'charming.'

"He was deaf, and she couldn't speak above a whisper. Therefore much of their communication was nonverbal or through writing. But one can express love and respect through nonverbal means. And this they had for each other— love and respect."

My wife, daughter Debbie, and I often think back to the time when we met Mrs. Matsuda at the Tokyo Lutheran Center.

Matsuda-san had suffered a loss that could easily have wrecked her personhood as thoroughly as it had destroyed her facial appearance. But her lifelong poise and dignity were unshaken. Her demeanor was telling us, "I shall not be greatly moved."

We had wondered whether she would have to communicate with us by means of writing. But we soon grew accustomed to her now small voice. We were surprised at her distinct pronunciation. With quiet strength and a light in her eye, she said,

"The doctors told me I would never be able to speak again. But they were wrong."

Again and again she reassured us about herself.

"I do not complain. I thank God that at 77 He allows me to do my own housework and take care of my eighty-year-old husband. I do not complain."

We told our 15-year-old Debbie, "You needn't stay. We can meet you later after we finish our visit with Matsuda-san."

But she insisted, "Dad, I want to stay."

And she listened with rapt attention as Matsuda-san praised God in the name of Jesus Christ for all His benefits to her. Our teen-ager was impressed with the strength and power of the spirit she was encountering in Matsuda-san.

When she was past 80 and was already deprived of her jawbone, Matsuda-san wrote us astonishing news.

"I began the study of German three years ago, and Russian two years ago. Memorizing new words is an almost insurmountable difficulty, as my memory is deteriorating with age. But it's a joy to study foreign languages, *n'est-ce pas? Nicht wahr?*"

Since foreign language lessons were broadcast in Tokyo, she made full use of the available educational opportunity just as she always had from her youth.

"At first I hesitated about trying to study Russian, as I felt I was not equal to studying such a difficult language — it being so different from any of the others I have studied.

There is little similarity in vocabulary with other languages. Young people may not find it so difficult to remember the new words and their suffixes according to cases. But it is a different story at my age.

"Yet the joy of studying helps me surmount the difficulties. In studying, as in all things, it is important to have some definite aim in view. I have, therefore, made it a rule to take the test the instructor gives at the end of each month. In order to write the answers, we must remember at least a certain amount of the words and phrases broadcast by the instructor.

"In this way I have managed to continue my study, which I do hope will help me avoid getting lazy in my old age."

Matsuda-san never finds time hanging heavy on her hands. She is never bored and finds little time for self-pity.

"Old people often complain of their loneliness, but I have got no time to complain. I'm always busy with something or other. I sometimes wish there were 34 hours in a day instead of 24."

A busy, determined person like Matsuda-san could never accept her afflictions with passive resignation. Let no Westerner imagine that Orientals don't feel suffering just exactly as we do. Let no American fancy that Matsuda-san naturally should be better able to endure great disappointment because of some unthinking stereotype of Japanese "fatalism."

"With what difficulty I speak and eat it's hard for me to tell you," she wrote recently. "But by God's help I've been able to bear the suffering."

She prays for healing as eagerly and importunately as any Western sufferer.

"My constant and persistent prayer is that God would

touch me with His healing hand, as He did Lazarus and the daughter of Jairus so many years ago.

"Yes, I firmly believe in miracles. And if it is His will, Jesus will help me get well.

"I sometimes feel my prayer is too persistent, but I just can't help doing so. He knows with what feeling I pray. Do join me in my prayer for my recovery!"

God has spared Matsuda-san's life through many operations. And that in itself is a compound miracle. But He has not given her the complete physical healing she has prayed for with such yearning. One can only imagine the spiritual struggles and tensions her faith has endured because she has not been fully healed.

Recently her condition has been worsening, and one of her letters says, "I'm too weak to write fully how much I am afflicted through being deprived of my speech. It's very hard to bear. Still I do not give up hope that God will make use of me in some way."

Matsuda-san has faith that God finds a purpose for her in this life even though she may appear useless to herself. Thus she overcomes one of the great temptations of elderly sufferers. And she refuses to despair.

"I'm getting shots for my mouth, and I still am praying that God will some day give me back my speech so that I may testify to people how merciful God is."

Matsuda-san prays to God with a persistence and determination that is much more characteristic of Oriental character than most Westerners imagine.

And yet she is ready to accept in faith His answer, "My grace is sufficient for you. My strength is made perfect in weakness."

That is the answer God gave Paul, the prince of missionaries, when he prayed the Lord three times to remove the thorn in his flesh. And Matsuda-san is ready to receive that answer, if it is His will.

With the selfsame Paul she can quietly say, "I can do all things through Christ who strengthens me. I have learned in whatever state I am to be therein content."

Arigata ya fusuma no

yuki mo

Jodo kara.

There are thanks to be given:

this snow on the bed quilt —

it too is from Heaven.

—Issa (1762 – 1826)

Cable from Tokyo

This book was written in a race against death.

Matsuda-san had provided much basic material and the story outline of her life. Her ability to express herself in English at the age of eighty was remarkable.

We turned her manuscript over to the publisher. After three months the verdict was, "This manuscript contains the material for a good book. But it should be rewritten with further background on the people who appear in the story and further explanations of things Japanese."

In the midst of a busy teaching schedule and while helping my colleagues fight for the life of our seminary, I sat down at my typewriter on October 2. Meanwhile, a stream of air mail letters was arriving from Tokyo. Matsuda-san had been hospitalized twice more. Her pleas for haste in publication became ever more urgent. She dearly wanted to see the book published before she was called home.

Till then her letters had been written in a firm round hand. But now her script was becoming unsteady and the words cramped. At the very least I wanted Mrs. Matsuda to see the finished manuscript, if not the book itself.

The publisher said, "If you can write the book in one month, we will have something on which to base a decision.

If it is acceptable, we can have the first copies out by late spring."

Resolutely, I put the seat of my pants on the seat of the chair.

To research, write, and rewrite with such intensity was in many ways an exhilarating experience. I felt myself drawn into the flow and surge of Matsuda-san and her times. She answered numerous questions in her letters. I felt myself borne up by her prayers. I was not carrying the work. The work was carrying me.

I was working in partnership with my co-author. Paradoxically, it was she who included most of the reference to American and English authors, while I was the one who sought to introduce the Japanese flavor and explain Oriental cultural references.

Our partnership was possible only because we had crossed the cultural bridge between Japan and America in both directions. Each had moved into the other's culture, though I cannot say that I have learned the Japanese language as well as she had mastered English.

A rich and varied worldwide exchange of gifts is in the making within the worldwide body of Christ.

The Japanese have a beautiful custom of *orei*. If one receives a favor, one shows appreciation by means of a gift. Matsuda-san's life story written in her 81st year is her *orei* to those who brought her God's strong Word, Jesus Christ.

Her experience points to unsuspected reserves of strength in God and in oneself to accept and overcome disease, misfortune, and death.

The greatest miracle is not healing from bodily disease, precious as this may be, but the creation of a new, redeemed person ripening in Christian faith and life.

It is a rare privilege to know such a mature Christian as Mrs. Matsuda. God healed and helped her and extended her life through 15 years of battling dread disease. In spite of all, God helped her attain the age of 81 and write her memoirs. But He gave her more than healing. Missionary Luther D. Kistler of the Lutheran Church in America, assistant pastor of her local congregation, commented on her spiritual depth and also wrote:

"She is a great lady and continues to witness to all of us with her dynamic faith."

After saying a final, deeply moving *Sayonara* to Mrs. Matsuda when last we were in Tokyo, I once more compared her with the devotees of the new religions in Japan. They had their millions of adherents, their imposing new headquarters. One such cathedral in Tokyo holds 30,000 worshipers. The Soka Gakkai has dedicated a magnificent new $100,000,000 Prayer Hall at the base of Mount Fuji. And the financial subscriptions were raised in just four days! This cult, which has grown from 1,500 adherents in 1945 to eight million today, can quote endless testimonials to success in love, business, and family problems. Its members can point to numerous dramatic healings.

Yet there is one miracle they cannot match. They cannot produce a Matsuda-san!

Were I to return to Japan as a missionary today, I would seek out the failures of the new religions, the poor unfortunates who were not healed and not helped. The same need and opportunity exist in the Christian West.

The new religions are for winners only. But Jesus Christ showed Matsuda-san how to win even when others thought she was losing. For that is what He Himself did on the cross and at the open tomb.

Mrs. Matsuda is profoundly grateful for the Christian witness she received from outstanding Japanese Christians assisted by able Western missionaries of various denominations. Every one of them enriched her. Her ripened life in Christ was a fruit of Christian unity in action.

I was impressed also with the role that Christian teachers and schools played in Matsuda-san's conversion and development.

Carol Kreyling's perceptive comment gave me pause:

"One thing that strikes me is the dominating influence of women in Mrs. Matsuda's life. This is interesting when one considers the traditional faulty interpretation of the role of woman and man in Japan. We who have lived in Japan for a long while know that it really is a very matriarchal society."

But amid all these meditations, I never lost sight for an instant of winning the race against death and getting at least the first draft of the manuscript to Matsuda-san in time.

The completed manuscript was handed to the publisher on November 2, just one month from the time the first line had been written. He was as pleasantly surprised as I was.

Another copy was sent at once by air mail to Tokyo. Eagerly, I awaited her response. Was Mrs. Matsuda still alive? Anxiously, I scanned the daily mail.

Finally, a blue air letter with an imprint of Japanese characters lay in my mailbox. The address in Matsuda-san's familiar hand reassured me. With God's help and her prayers we had won the race against death!

It was gratifying to receive her accolade. "I'm glad you've succeeded in bringing out the atmosphere I've desired."

Under date of November 27 I was able to write Matsuda-san the good news that the publisher had officially accepted the story of her life.

On November 28, she wrote a brief letter indicating great weariness. "I'm going to the hospital for consultation on Friday, December 1. Can't write any longer. Hoping the book will soon be put in print. Your friend in Christ, Kiyoko Matsuda."

Missionary Luther Kistler wrote on the very same day: "Mrs. Matsuda will enter Ochanomizu Hospital again this Friday to have some sort of instrument inserted to help her swallow. Recently her throat has become rather constricted, and she is hardly able to swallow anything. Her condition seems to be generally weaker, but we can never underestimate her determination. However, she doesn't seem able to rally this time."

But, characteristically, she was still thinking first of others. Pastor Kistler went on:

"I was really impressed today when she very much wanted to introduce me to a neighbor, an American lady married to a Japanese man. She thought it would be good for this lady to make the acquaintance of another American. Mrs. Matsuda insisted on walking with me up the street to meet the lady. So we went and had a very nice little visit. Needless to say, Mrs. Matsuda tried very hard to speak, and we could understand her a little bit. Today most of the time she wrote everything down for me when we talked together at her house. Even her handwriting is getting more difficult to read.

"What seems to be giving her the most pleasure now is knowing that her history is under way and may be published." She knew it could help other people.

On December 4 my phone rang. It was 11:00 a. m.

"This is Western Union. We have a cable for you from Tokyo: MRS. MATSUDA DIED DECEMBER 1. THANKS FOR KINDNESS WHILE LIVED. MATSUDAS."

I glanced at my watch. With Tokyo fourteen hours ahead of St. Louis, the funeral had already taken place. They had taken her frail remains to the crematorium in the customary wooden coffin of plain, unfinished pine. Already, the dark smoke had curled from the tall chimney into the smog-laden air of Greater Tokyo. But in the face of these grim realities the stronger reality of Jesus Christ and His victorious resurrection had been spoken.

Matsuda-san would not now be able to present a copy of her life story personally to the wife of the *Mainichi* newspaper editor in Tokyo. But God would find other witnesses to take up tasks like that.

I breathed a prayer of thanks to God for having known Mrs. Matsuda, and her stalwart faith and courageous example, for the witness she would continue to make through the story of her life, and for God's help in winning the race against death—with only three weeks to spare.

Picking up the phone I dictated a cable in reply: SYMPATHY TO FAMILY. THANKSGIVING FOR GREAT CHRISTIAN PERSON.

And softly I added,

"Sayonara—if it must be so."

May she rest in peace, and may Light Eternal shine upon her.